OVERTHINKING

Become Focused, Decluttered and Motivated to
Achieve Your Goals

(Discover Small Habits to Fight Anxiety and
Reduce Stress)

Ray Fowler

Published by Knowledge Icons

Ray Fowler

Overthinking: Become Focused, Decluttered and Motivated to Achieve Your Goals (Discover Small Habits to Fight Anxiety and Reduce Stress)

ISBN 978-1-990084-66-9

Legal & Disclaimer

The information contained in this book is not designed to replace or take the place of any form of medicine or professional medical advice. The information in this book has been provided for educational and entertainment purposes only.

The information contained in this book has been compiled from sources deemed reliable, and it is accurate to the best of the Author's knowledge; however, the Author cannot guarantee its accuracy and validity and cannot be held liable for any errors or omissions. Changes are periodically made to this book. You must consult your doctor or get professional medical advice before using any of the suggested remedies, techniques, or information in this book.

Upon using the information contained in this book, you agree to hold harmless the Author from and against any damages, costs, and expenses, including any legal fees potentially resulting from the application of any of the information provided by this guide. This disclaimer applies to any damages or injury caused by the use and application, whether directly or indirectly, of any advice or information presented, whether for breach of contract, tort, negligence, personal injury, criminal intent, or under any other cause of action.

You agree to accept all risks of using the information presented inside this book. You need to consult a professional medical practitioner in order to ensure you are both able and healthy enough to participate in this program.

TABLE OF CONTENTS

Introduction

The following chapters will discuss Overthinking, which as its name suggests, thinking too much and long about the anxiety-inducing occurrence, usually but not always a negative experience of some kind (e.g., past mistake, current concern, or future outcome). Do you find it hard to shut down your racing mind? Do you feel fatigued and troubled because of your thoughts? If so, you are likely an acute overthinker. Today, overthinking is an international epidemic, since we live in difficult and demanding times that require so much mental capacity from us to function and succeed in. Adult responsibilities, money, mental trauma, and other problems leave our minds active 24/7. After thorough research, psychology professor Susan Nolen-Hoeksema from the University of Michigan found that young and middle-aged adults are especially prone to overthinking with 73% of 25-35-

year-olds identified as overthinkers. Unsurprisingly, more women (57%) than men (43%) identify themselves as overthinkers; men are more likely to distract or detach themselves from their thoughts and feelings. So, if you have trouble controlling your thoughts and feel weighed down by them, this book will provide you an overview and guide to stop overthinking and recognize the subtle signs of overthinking. Now that you know what overthinking is, it is important to emphasize that overthinking is not inherently negative or wrong. Everyone automatically overthinks from time to time due to the hectic and demanding nature of modern life (e.g., Mortgage, career expectations, children, finances, etc.). With that being said, there comes the point when everything, especially future decisions can lead to unknown anxiety and negative outcomes; at which point, doing nothing is preferable to taking a risk and facing the unknown consequences of your decisions. At this point, overthinking becomes a problem.

The next question is how to assess and solve the unconscious problem of overthinking. Firstly, it is important to understand what causes overthinking. Beyond mental issues such as depression and anxiety, other contributing factors include experiencing childhood abuse, neglect, a traumatic event, being a perfectionist, having a genetic predisposition, and introversion. Using the following checklist, you can determine if you meet the threshold for overthinking or not: the need for perfectionism, insomnia, burnout, requiring others feedback on unimportant matters, irritability, occasional hypochondriasis, consistent sadness/negative thinking, and a believed lack of control over parts of life.

After realizing that you suffer from overthinking, you've taken the first step towards resolving the problem. The next steps are to recognize cognitive biases, identify which ones apply most to you, be conscious of your thought processes all through the day, challenge your knee-jerk thoughts and replace your cognitive biases with reality. If necessary, consider professional psychiatric help to overcome mental health issues, especially if you've suffered from childhood abuse.

In order to keep overthinking at bay and find peace of mind, consider adopting a stoic approach to life, break negative thought habits, engage in meditation and relaxation techniques to calm the mind, and sleep well. Also, be sure to cultivate positive energies and thinking into your life to prevent yourself from overthinking. This is best accomplished through loving yourself by learning the true meaning of this cliché phrase and how it differs from narcissism; with self-love being about valuing and taking regard for your own happiness and well-being and narcissism defined by its excessive vanity need for admiration from others to cover up one's own insecurities and low-self-esteem about themselves. Lastly, it is vital to always have in mind that you can conquer overthinking and to accept yourself, in spite of all your flaws because you are not the sum of all your mistakes or failures. There are plenty of books on this subject on the market, thanks again for choosing this one! Every effort was made to ensure it is full of as much useful information as possible, and please enjoy it!

Chapter 1: Cause And Principles Of

Overthinking

Again, there is nothing wrong about thinking about your problems so you can think of a solution for them, it becomes worrisome when you have a bad habit of twisting narratives around in your head until you can see every angle and side to it. Overthinking is not productive as it just makes you dwell over your problems; you are not looking for a solution for them and you are only making yourself feel miserable.

In order to find an effective way to break your overthinking habit, you need to find out what caused it in the first place. Below are some of the more common reasons as to why people tend to overthink their problems rather than actually find a solution for them.

Information overload

If you are not self-confident, you tend to doubt every little thing that you say or do. When you hesitate, even a little, about the things that you want to do, you are letting uncertainty and fear creep into your mind, and it will be very difficult to get them out of there. You can never really tell what your decisions will take you; even if you planned every little detail, the outcome will still not be exactly what you hoped for (it could either be better or worse than what you planned). This is why you should learn to take risks and not torture yourself when you did not get the results you wished for.

When You Worry Too Much

It is only natural to worry when you encounter new and unfamiliar things and events. However, if you worry too much that you cannot even imagine a positive outcome, then it will trigger you to overthink. This is problematic because worry attracts even more problems; sometimes it creates ones out of thin air, which cause overthinking to go even deeper. Instead of mulling over how things could go wrong, it is better to entertain thoughts that are more positive, like how much better you would feel if a certain even turns in your favor.

When You Overthink to Protect Yourself

Some people believe that they can protect themselves from troubles whenever they overthink, but the truth is that overthinking is a trap that kills your progress. Overthinking and not doing anything to change the status quo might seem good, but stifling your progress is never a good thing at all. In addition, when you overthink, you are not really staying at the same position, you are actually undoing whatever amount of progress you achieved thus far.

You are Unable to "Turn Off" Your Mind

Many over thinkers became that way because they cannot seem to get their minds off their problems no matter how hard they try. People who are sensitive to stress live as if they are constantly wound up tightly, they have somehow forgotten how to relax and change their chain of thoughts. Overthinking happens when a person stresses too much on a single problem, and he could not turn his focus away from it.

You are Always Chasing after Perfection

Being a perfectionist is not necessarily a good thing. In fact, one could argue that being a perfectionist is not good at all. Most people who struggle with perfectionism are constantly anxious. They often wake up in the middle of the night thinking of the things that they could have done better. Being a perfectionist causes overthinking because you are always trying to outdo yourself.

Overthinking is Your Habit

Overthinking is not always caused by a person's bad habits; sometimes overthinking IS the person's bad habit. For some people, it does not take much for them to overthink; they usually default to overthinking the moment that they encounter even minor inconvenience. This bad habit prevents people from living their lives the way they actually wanted to.

Fear

You can never completely curb your anxiety unless you face the fears it is rooted in. You can only feel strong when you master your emotions of fear and apprehensiveness, and this can only be possible if you actually face that to which you are afraid.

Now that you are aware of how to control your negative thoughts and be mindful of how you feel, consciously make a list of everything that you are afraid of doing. Things such as confronting your feelings to your crush, starting your own business, publishing your book, trying adventure sports, and anything else that you feel is holding you back can go on that list.

Once your list is ready, pick any one fear that you would like to overcome first and create a plan of action to curb it. If you are afraid of speaking publicly but have always wanted to pursue it, prepare a short speech on a topic you are passionate about and practice speaking it for a minute or two in front of the mirror, close friend or just by yourself.

Once you have **command over it**, speak on the topic in front of 2 to 3 people. You may stumble and make mistakes, but if you do manage to stay strong in that time, you will overcome a part of your fear. Slowly keep speaking in front of more people and soon enough, you will have overcome your fear.

After **overcoming one little fear**, take on another one, and then another one. Keep combatting your fears this way and thwart them one after another to have better control of your emotions and master them. Remember to record your daily activities and performance in a journal so that you can go through the accounts time and again. This gives insight into your strengths, mistakes, setbacks and accomplishments so that you feel motivated on acknowledging your accomplishments, learn from your mistakes, and improve on them to only do better the next time.

Chapter 2: Different Causes Of Over-

Thinking

These days overthinking diverse life circumstances and other easygoing things is an across the board issue. It does not imply that instructing yourself or thinking over your issues is something awful, however on the off chance that you have a propensity to bend everything around in your mind until you see it in each point and plausibility, at that point you are an over-thinker. Thinking over different things and occasions is a characteristic

piece of life for some individuals. It, as a rule, causes individuals to discover arrangements of their issues and prepares them to confront life challenges and overcome obstructions.

There is an incredible assortment of focal points and disservices of being an over-thinker. Do you prefer to know the reasons why those irritating considerations about different issues cause you to overthink? Peruse on to discover a couple of irrefutable reasons why you overthink your issues.

1. You can't unwind

It frequently turns out that you cannot get your psyche off the issue you cannot quit thinking about. Numerous delicate individuals live in consistent strain since they do not have the foggiest idea of how to unwind and supplant the chain of negative musings by positive ones. The most ideal way to divert yourself from overthinking is to practice or do yoga. Yoga is an ideal apparatus to quiet your rich creative mind down and alleviation your stresses over the issue. Simply take a sit and envision a glad spot that makes you feel certain, free and fulfilled.

2. A steady worrier

Stressing is a characteristic response to new and obscure things. As indicated by various looks into numerous youngsters are worriers essentially. They frequently think that it is hard to envision how things can go right. These individuals pull in issues since they want to attract horrendous pictures of their psyches. It is alluring to concentrate on positive musings and thoughts on the best way to achieve your objectives than thinking about your disappointments. It is conceivable to change your qualities of character and propensities, and you will be able to sufficiently overcome stresses. Do your best to turn into a hopeful person and create a constructive vision of the world.

3. Absence of certainty

Absence of certainty is one of the primary things which cause the issue of overthinking. When you dither about things you do, you let vulnerability and dread fill your brain. No one can tell where your choices will lead you, that is the reason you should go out on a limb without tormenting yourself. When you begin making choices, you will consequently help your certainty. When you are certain and solid, you will overcome all troubles without making a decent attempt.

4. Overthinking is only an inclination

Overthinking your issues and steady research of your activities frequently transform into an unfortunate propensity. This propensity more often than not keeps you stuck from having a glad existence. It is very hard to end this mind-desensitizing propensity, yet you ought to consistently attempt to discover yourself overthinking and change these irritating considerations. When you feel that your mind starts to deliver a dramatization, you ought to possess yourself on some fascinating and including action. It will enable you to overcome overthinking. Thinking is an inescapable piece of your life that causes you to achieve objectives and keep away from inconveniences, however, you should realize the contrast among thinking and overthink. The inclination to overthink issues can negatively affect your wellbeing.

5. Overthinking is a security

Some of the time individuals accept that overthinking can be a sort of security from inconveniences. The snare of overthinking is slaughtering your advancement. There is more profit by activity than from inaction since encounters make you progressively develop and more grounded. Overthinking grows both your insurance and the opportunity to lose an open door since your mind is continually discussing the circumstance, scrabbling for another arrangement.

6. You need to be immaculate

You ought to know about the way that the expenses of being a stickler are high. Numerous individuals who battle with compulsiveness generally live inclination on edge constantly. Hairsplitting causes overthinking since sticklers consistently attempt to improve. They may likewise wake up amidst the night thinking about what should be finished. Such a way of life can without much of a stretch harm your psychological and physical prosperity. You ought to comprehend that no one's ideal and it is smarter to dispose of the propensity for overthinking everything.

7. Re-thinking yourself

It is smarter to settle on choices all the more effectively and rapidly. You should simply to dispose of the propensity to re-think yourself. Re-thinking makes you audit the circumstance over and over in your brain since you have a hunch that you have not done things appropriately. Subsequently, you are forever discontent or substance that you have settled on the correct decision. Attempt to be progressively certain about yourself and in your capacities. It will enable you to be less fixated on your easygoing choices as the day progressed.

Chapter 3: Problem Solving Strategies

Set It and Forget It
The advice to 'Set It and Forget It' will come up over and over again in your life. You probably first learned this as a child, watching your parents make not of dental appointments, items needed for a camping trip, and so on. At some point, you started keeping a calendar of sorts. We have all learned if you have an important appointment, deadline, meeting, or haircut you write it down on your calendar and don't worry about it anymore.

The same holds true for these worry loops. When angst over an issue starts to turn over in your head, get that pad and pen and turn to a new page. Write that conversation loop down word for word. Then write down your new arguments, feelings, the way you had wished it had turned out, etc. Keep writing until you have let go of the loop and can move on with the rest of your day.

Always end your writing with a few lines of affirmation such as:

I can deal with this problem

I can move on from one-sided relationships that drain me of energy

I can create my own joy and happiness

If I don't know the answer, I can find it

I can ask for help if I need some

I am making my life less complicated

Lack of Sleep

Insomnia is a problem with people who overthink. You're beaten. All you want to do is fall into a sound sleep. Boing! A loop starts. Again, write it down and keep writing until you can't think of another word to say. Tell your mind that this is exactly like the calendar and you won't forget your side of the argument tomorrow when the worry comes back. It's all down on paper and it is safe for your brain to think and dream about other topics.

If the loop clicks back on when you click the light off, start again. Write every word that pops into your head. It might be as odd as, "... I can't believe I can't get to sleep. Why did he say that and what did he mean? Now I wonder if he is trying to tell me someone else would be better to lead that project. I really thought I was doing a great job ..." and so on.

At some point in your midnight ramble, you will hit on what it is that is bothering you and robbing you of your much-needed rest. Then star that line or those lines that seem most likely to be the source of your anxiety and leave them until morning.

~ What you believe you deserve is what you get in life. Change your beliefs and your life transforms. ~

- Jaclyn Nicole Johnston

Listing and Journaling

Many self-help articles and books advise the reader to start journaling. This is great advice, only many readers ignore it because they don't really know what journaling is, or how to start. They are not writers and feel foolish at the thought of emoting on the page.

You don't need to be an award-winning journalist to the journal. As a matter of fact, if you have done any of the exercises above, you have already started journaling. What is meant by journaling in this instance is to write down occurrences of overthinking when they happen. Note details such as the time, place, where you with anyone, or what were you discussing? Did you see someone or something that set off a loop? All of this information will help you figure out what is setting you off and help you shut the loop down.

If you ever took any kind of chemistry or biology lab, you had to keep a notebook, it can be that dry. Date. Location. Time of Day. Record your thoughts, actions, solutions, worry loops, exercises, ideas for changing routines, or a list.

Listing is also helpful. If you don't want to record sentences. List feelings, items you might need to solve a problem, places that calm you, locations you would like to visit, adventures you would like to try. Don't limit yourself, daydream and ride that camel in the desert.

There is a reason your mind is going to this place, churning through the thought or problem. That is what makes journaling or listing so powerful. Give the idea on the page its own time and audience. Come back to these pages in a week or a month and see what they mean to you then.

Much of overcoming negative, worry loops and overthinking is about learning to trust again. To trust your decisions, your ability to cope with problems when they arise. To trust yourself not to barrel down the wrong path with no plan or perpetrations.

That is what the exercises and surveys in this book are designed to help. Refusing to work in negative atmospheres or environments. Setting boundaries to negative people at bay. Finding close friends who will not judge you for your shortcomings and will help you with your healing. It doesn't take many.

~ The greatest win is walking away and choosing not to engage in drama and toxic energy at all. ~

- Lalah Delia

Learning to Let Go ~ Deal With the Problem

Learning to let go might be the hardest part of the entire process for some. When a routine has been put in place to deal with a problem, we don't want to change that routine. Change is difficult. Scary. We may have developed some bad habits as part of our routine. Eating, smoking, drinking, etc. All of those are temporary fixes to make us feel a little better about the problem we are avoiding.

There it is, the other shoe dropped. The overthinking allows us to avoid dealing with uncomfortable situations, people, or facts.

Let look at some possible answers as to why we are avoiding these situations we find so uncomfortable.

Nothing in Moderation

Think back to our list of signs of anxiety. 'People who overthink have a tendency to see the world as black and white ... go all in every time ... leads to feelings of inadequacy and self-doubt that can fuel depression ...'

Here is a classic example of avoidance that most readers will recognize.

Let's meet Grace, our thirty-something over-thinker. Grace is smart, has a rising career, is artistic, and is finally taking time to work on her personal life. She is funny, enjoys travel, and is always up for a challenge. Grace puts up a good front, but she is very shy.

Grace started her personal makeover with a change in exercise, which is where she meets Ivy. Ivy is married, has several children, is very fit, and fun. She has fascinating friends, gives great parties, and she makes everyone feel special.

But there was another side to both women that the public doesn't see. Ivy is stuck in a loveless marriage and Grace has been so career-oriented she has no personal life.

It seems like a perfect friendship. Ivy and Grace both like movies, theater, and participate in sporting events. They meet for workouts, have get-togethers with other friends. But in reality, along with the friendship is some **avoidance of problems** by both women.

It turns out that Grace is a great distraction from Ivy's failing marriage and all the fun times with Ivy and her friends make Grace feel like she has a life.

Grace feels like Ivy is pulling away and starts overthinking comments made by Ivy. She starts to feel used like she is a reason for Ivy to get out of the house and away from the family. Meanwhile, Ivy is getting kind of irritated with Grace wanting to be included in everything. Ivy is moving on and getting a divorce, and Grace hasn't started dating anyone.

They are attracted to the same men. Grace gets angry and jealous because Ivy has such ease at making friends. The friendship ends up dissolving and **Grace doesn't understand why it's happened again**. She has been through this friendship fallout before. Sometimes she pulls away, sometimes the other person pulls away. Doesn't happen with every friendship, only when she feels like she's on the verge of being truly happy. Then it gets snatched away.

~ We must have a pie. Stress cannot exist in the presence of a pie. ~

- David Mamet, Boston Marriage

Stressed Relationships

You can see clearly in the case of Grace and Ivy, Grace puts a strain on the friendship by deciding that Ivy would help her develop the social life she had always wanted. Ivy did not ask for or want the job of helping Grace with her anxieties.

Make a list of your close friends and family. If you have that feeling that some have been pulling away, write down when you first noticed the distancing. Note what was going on. Where you at a BBQ, over for a chat, someone's birthday. Friendships take work.

Make sure you are giving as much of your time and effort as you are getting from your friends and family. Give your time, listen to the stories of their ups and downs, and surprise them with little gifts on the odd occasion. Dropping a note in the mail letting someone know you are thinking about them is a wonderful way to strengthen a friendship.

Make up a reminder list of things to think about each week and tape it next to the bathroom mirror or somewhere you will see it daily. Nothing exotic, just something to remind you to remember friends and family in little ways.

Is there someone's birthday coming up?

Who has a special event that needs to be honored?

Extra support for kids this week?

Planning for a holiday?

Treats for a gathering?

If you feel like you have a relationship that is strained, and you are caught in worry loops and feel like you are always doing the heavy lifting in trying to keep the friendship up. Stop. Take a step back. Think about trying one of the following instead of sitting and stewing.

Coping Strategies

Plan a Date - If you thought you had a good time planned with your friend and it falls through. Don't start second-guessing and wondering what's going on. Either goes on with the plans you had made or deliberately do something else. You will probably see someone you know, or meet someone new. Even if it's not as much fun, you are exercising new social muscles and it gets much easier each time you set your own schedule. And before you know it, you don't need to rely on anyone else because you have a social life.

Take a Walk - If you are feeling overwhelmed by a situation. Take a quick walk to clear your head and get your blood pumping. Deliberately find something else to think about during that walk.

Take a Nap - Stress can wear you out. If you are so wound up about something and it is eating up your time by preventing you from functioning. Stop. Grab a good book, put on some soothing music, and read yourself to sleep.

Deep Breaths - When you realize that you are in the grips of an overthinking moment. Stop. Inhale in for 3 counts and exhale for 6 counts. Do that about five times. You will calm down and lower your blood pressure. Then choose a method from one of the earlier exercises and try to figure out what is at the heart of that anxiety.

Drift Away - At some point, you have to let go completely. You need to acknowledge that you are using an event, friendship, job, to avoid dealing with one or more issues. For example, you may be trying to make more out of your job than is in your job description. So, stop fussing and fretting about your current job and go find that job you really want.

Distract yourself - Sometimes we just need to set our brains in neutral and go with the flow. It doesn't have to be a long break, but it needs to engage a different part of the brain so that you are busy enough to break any stress or anxiety and come back to what you were doing with a clear head and fresh eyes. Watch a silly video, take a yoga class, play sports, listen to music, clean something, write a letter, garden, paint your nails, play a card game, read a magazine, good book, or a joke book.

Create - Stuck in a rut and your brain is running away with some sad sack situation and you are trapped. Crank up a different part of your brain and stretch your imagination. Write a story, poem, or thank you note, draw cartoons, paint a picture, plan a garden - you don't have to plant it, doodle on paper while humming your favorite song.

Inspire Yourself - Make a feel-good moment in the day. It could be as simple as leaving a little note for a loved one or a thank you note for a co-worker. Do something to make yourself feel good. Think of something happy, do something kind, give someone a hug, write a positive note, read inspirational quotes, write down five things you love about yourself.

Play - Make time out to play once in a while. You never know what it will lead to, but it will probably be fun. You will also find that you will learn to work playtime into your schedule and that of your friends or family more easily as time goes by. Sometimes people are discouraged from playing when they leave the schoolyard.

Nonsense. Living life to the fullest includes playtime. Plan a fun trip, cook or bake, go for a walk and take pictures, skip, jump rope, blow bubbles, play with clay or silly putty.

When Other's Stress Becomes Yours

Another trap to look out for is allowing someone else's stress to become yours.

You want to be able to deal with situations compassionately and with understanding. But there is a limit. Don't let yourself get sucked into a bad situation not of your own making when there is nothing more you can do to help.

There are different levels of stress and dysfunction you may experience in your life from friends, family, and co-workers. From passive-aggressive, almost childish avoidance of issues to frightening episodes where someone may be putting their own lives in danger.

Let's say you and your best friend have decided to share a room and board at college. Your friend is smart, charming, and witty. He has a fun circle of friends and keeps everyone in stitches with his antics. What you didn't know about your roommate is that he has a dark side that doesn't come out until you started rooming together. He sinks into dark moods where he won't communicate, is unwilling to clean up after himself, and will not take on the responsibility of cleaning, cooking, etc.

At first, you think it is simply a phase he is going through, and then you start to realize it is a bit more than basic stress of college, exams, and social pressures. You cannot make him do his chores or treat you with respect and kindness. All you can do is remind him of the house rules and boundaries and see how he performs for the rest of the semester. If he doesn't shape up, do not renew the lease with him. Find a new roommate or a new place to stay. That seems harsh but you cannot do the work for him forever. Suggest that he see a doctor, or that he needs to let his parents know he is having difficulties, but that's about all you can do. Do not keep trying to solve his problems and wait for him to change. Why should he when you are doing all the work?

Learn when to take a step back and let go.

There was a graduate student who had battled manic-depressive cycles for as long as she at been at the college. She had come from a difficult home with a stepfather and three older stepbrothers. There were definite signs of abuse, but none of her friends recognized the signs of this type of emotional disturbance.

The university system was not very well equipped to deal with emotional trauma at this level. And there wasn't much in the way of emotional help for students suffering from any kind of disorder. Her friends tried to help her through bad moods and angry fits, one which included some broken glass and a visit from campus police, with little success.

The student tried to open up about the abuse without much success - shame is a strong emotion and often keeps people from seeking the help they need. Fortunately, she was able to invite friends to come with her on short trips back home. The student knew she would be okay if she was not alone in the house. Her friends were unaware of the violence she had faced at home but knew their presence was a comfort.

Though extremely bright, and capable when she was not on a down-swing, she slowly spiraled out of control. Friends urged her to see a doctor, with not much success. The situation came to a head when the student tried to commit suicide and was discharged from school. Her friends had watched her go from a successful student to an out-of-control person they hardly recognized. It wasn't until a few months before the attempted suicide that her friends began to understand how serious her problems were and how out of their depth, they were in dealing with the problem.

At the time, there was no 911 and mental health was not a topic of discussion for polite company. Thankfully some things have changed and most people have a basic understanding of the difference between the blues and an actual emotional order that needs attention.

Unfortunately, even if you do recognize the signs of emotional trauma, if your friend doesn't or is in denial there is really nothing you can do. He or she may reject all your help or suggestions. You can urge them to seek help, but if they don't believe they are ill they won't go. All you can do is trying, but at some point, you must let go.

You can ask your friend to go with you to see a counselor. Turn the situation around and let her know that you need humoring.

You need the doctor to tell you that your friend is okay and not in any emotional trauma.

If you reach a point where your friend is threatening suicide call 911. It seems extreme, but new eyes will be on the problem and your friend might get the help he or she needs.

Chapter 4: How To Identify If You Are An

Overthinker

The biggest cause of unhappiness is overthinking.

A big gap exists between deliberating and solving problems. Some often suggest that women are more likely to overthink than men, but the truth is that no one manages to avoid overthinking; it is something everyone does.

A therapist meets with thousands of individuals in their office daily, many of whom are searching for help in dealing with overthinking. Many often complain about their inability to relax. They feel that their brain is constantly preoccupied with worries and negative thoughts, and, as a result, they feel so much anxiety that they can't rest. Some complain about the fact that they focus excessively on how much better their lives would be without the mistakes they have made.

There is a strong connection between overthinking and mental health problems, such as anxiety and depression. Those suffering from overthinking might not even notice the decline in their mental health because they are so preoccupied and worried; they are not living in the mindfully. Such individuals might feel that their overthinking is healthy and useful, and without it some horrible calamity might happen.

But the truth is just the opposite. Overthinking increases the chances of feeling lost, anxious, and miserable. It can also lead to resentment and anger that clouds your judgment and makes it hard for you to make the right decisions. This state is often referred to as analysis paralysis.

Forms of Overthinking

Overthinking keeps reminding you of things you can't control, such as your failure. There are basically two forms of overthinking, namely: an excessive rumination on the past and worrying excessively about future events. These preoccupations prevent you from making progress in your life. There is a clear difference between overthinking, self-reflection, and problem-solving.

How is overthinking different from problem-solving? There is a clear difference between problem-solving and overthinking. When problem-solving, your goal is to solve an underlying problem. Overthinkers dwell more on the problems themselves than possible solutions to their problems.

How about self-reflection? Is it the same as overthinking? No! Self-reflection has a definite purpose; it helps you discover new things about yourself, your condition, and your situation.

What's the bottom line? While you are overthinking, you're not productive. However, self-reflection and problem-solving help you create solutions and recognize behaviors that may be holding you back.

Are You an Overthinker?

We all have a tendency to overthink. Being aware of this fact makes it easier to change. And the first step involves identifying the damage caused by overthinking.

The idea that overthinking stops bad things from happening is a subconscious perception nurtured by many; they feel that the failure to ruminate over past events will precipitate some sort of unforeseen calamity. Research indicates that overthinking is not healthy and will impact our lives negatively.

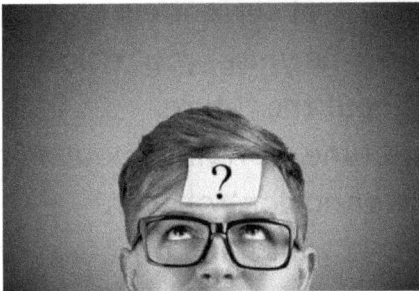

Ten Signs That You Are an Overthinker

Consider the following signs that show you're overthinking:

You repeatedly mentally revisit embarrassing moments in your head.

You find it difficult to sleep because your brain just won't shut off.

You ask yourself numerous questions, such as: What if?

You spend time thinking about the hidden meanings in events and social interactions.

You repeat past conversations you have had with others and think about things that you should or shouldn't have said.

You always remember your mistakes.

You keep playing a script of what someone did or said that you're angry about.

You lose track of current events happening around you because you're lost in deep thought about the future.

You spend time worrying about things you have little or no control over.

You can't rid your mind of your worries.

If you notice the tendency to become enmeshed in overthinking, don't despair. You can use the strategies below to get back your energy, time, and brainpower.

From proper time scheduling to thought substitution, here are several exercises that will boost your mental strength and help you stop overthinking everything.

Things Overthinkers Do (That They Never Talk About)

If you are an overthinker, you limit your chances of becoming successful in life. It will prevent you from reaching your goals and make your life miserable.

Below are ten of the things overthinkers do without paying attention to;

They apologize excessively

When you tell an overthinker that they have wronged you, before even identifying if the situation is their fault, they start to apologize. This leaves them exposed to additional criticism, which may or may not be warranted.

It is good to accept blame and reduce others' tension sometimes, but if this is done exclusively to please others, or because you're scared of what they will think about you, it is unhealthy.

An overthinker always wants to smooth things over with other people. This causes them more pain in the long run.

Critical thinking is their thing

Most overthinkers are excellent critical thinkers. This is one of the excellent things about overthinking. An overthinker spends all of their time deliberating and analyzing each decision in an unending manner. Therefore, they often come up with the best results.

Overthinkers can punch their way out of a paper bag, but only after analyzing the entire makeup of the bag, and the soft spots. That takes a whole lot of time, but they deliver the best results. Often, overthinkers use their tunnel vision to focus relentlessly on a problem until they come up with a solution.

Sleeping is an issue.

An overthinker's brain never stops working. It keeps spinning at maximum speed all day long. This makes them restless, and sleeping becomes impossible. Their minds refuse to shut down, even when their body needs sleep.

They worry excessively about making others happy.

Overthinkers forget that they should be happy too. They worry about others' happiness, forgetting they need to be happy. They often negatively exaggerate how the world will view their feelings, actions, thoughts, decisions, and words.

This limits their progress and makes accomplishing their personal goals harder. They make decisions that please others, instead of themselves.

Overthinkers May Also Be Escape Artists.

In order to escape their own minds, overthinkers might resort to overworking, excessive activity, perfectionism, and other extreme habits to escape from their overthinking.

Those with more serious issues may turn to state-altering medications or drugs to take the edge off.

They experience severe headaches or migraines.

Catastrophic overthinking may cause somatization, such as headaches, stomachaches, etc. Those especially prone to worrying or overthinking may fear that their headache is a symptom of something more serious, which may make their headache even worse.

They research their purchases excessively or always need a second opinion.

When making purchases, those that overthink may become paralyzed with the overabundance of options that are available to them. They may search online for hours for the best options. They may ask all of their friends' opinions.

When shopping, they may need to consider multiple options or ask a friend to come along just to approve their choice. This comes from a place of low self-confidence. They wait for others to decide or approve what they will eat, wear, and do.

Their overthinking stems from insecurity.

They often overthink because they are unsure of their decisions; this makes it hard for them to decide on what to do. At work, they might have issues choosing clients, projects, or the best course of action to take when problems arise. This lack of confidence can lead them to be doubted by others, even when they end up making the right decisions.

They may become overly preoccupied.

They may not be able to see the forest for the trees. When they become overly preoccupied, they may miss important dates or appointments.

They may search endlessly for reasons to stop overthinking.

Some often admit that they overthink; it may be something that they always try to break free from. They may overthink about ways to stop overthinking.

19 Things You Need to Stop Overthinking

Specifically, while there are a lot of things that people overthink about, there are some aspects of life that a person shouldn't even waste his or her time thinking about.

Let's check them out one by one.

Whether You Love or You Don't Love Someone

That shouldn't be rocket science. Because, finally, you either do or do not. For sure, whether you love the person or not, you will eventually know.

If the One Who You Love is The One You Will Want Forever

There is no genuine or sincere timeline; the only timeline is the stereotype that society portrays today. When you don't follow it, it might make you feel ashamed. For a lifelong decision, you don't have to be sure right away; many people aren't sure right away, either.

Mundane Social Discrepancies

You fear that people do not want to talk with/to you; as a result, you worry or think they don't want to hang out with you. No, that isn't necessarily the case. Sometimes, people don't have the time. So, don't panic automatically. The only time it means something is when someone says to your face that they aren't into you.

How You Appear to Others

How people view you depends on the filter that they view you through. This includes their own biases and beliefs about others. What they think and feel about you will seem accurate to them, but it might not reflect the real you. Know yourself and be positive.

The Difference Between What Someone Says and What They Mean

People don't always mean what they say! It can sometimes be easy for you to identify when they aren't entirely honest with you. Yes, it's a gut feeling; their body language speaks volumes. However, sometimes people will not be honest with you, and you will have to take them at their word, or not at all.

The Grand Scheme of Things

Have you ever thought about how grand the whole world is? At a point, do you feel like proceeding? Certainly not! The vastness and mightiness of the universe, on the other hand, is awe-inspiring, and spending time to understand the details is an interesting but unproductive use of our imaginations.

Your Exact Place in the World

Don't compare yourself to anyone. Where you are right now is your place. If you want to change, your subsequent destination is your new place. When it comes to where one needs to be in life, there is no right and wrong answer.

Whether You Are Happy or Not

When you are overthinking about whether you are happy or not, you are not satisfied. Do you feel you delighted? If answering that is tough, then you are not happy.

Whether You Have Made a Bad Decision or Not

If you keep dwelling on past choices, you will not change anything in your future. The right thing to think about is the step that you should take next.

Whether you should meet up with someone and hang out

You have many assumptions in your head: Will they say no, yes, or maybe? Will they reject you outright? Chances are they don't know what's in your mind. So, what's healthy here is give it a try. They might feel flattered and happy that you want to spend time with them and strengthen the relationship.

Every minute detail about why some things didn't work out

The moment has passed! You will not get the chance to work these things out now. So, let them go! For the sake of growth, you could reflect on those occasions, so you don't make the same mistakes again. However, when you overthink them, you will bury yourself in sadness and remorse.

How society will define you

Society's labels don't define you. They are simply what people use to identify you. You do not have to use them to identify yourself.

Jokes

Sadly, many people overthink an excellent joke and become upset. They should just try to enjoy it. Overthinking jokes saps your joy. So, don't worry about what's behind everything that some people say.

Higher spiritual and deeper philosophical meanings behind everything.

Most times, we don't need to know. And you will never know for sure, unfortunately.

Writing an email

You should not re-read emails excessively before sending them. Imagine spending hours wondering if your email would make sense. Should you write it this way? I'm not saying one shouldn't think about this at all, but you should only spend a few moments composing and fine-tuning your message. So, while you need to be conscious of your words, don't overthink to the point that you will have to discard the idea of sending the mail entirely.

What your social media presence reveals about you

I'm impressed by people who do not usually post pictures of their success and achievements on social media. It tells me that they are out there, living their lives and enjoying them, and that they are not sidetracked with what goes on around them. Also, it shows they immersed in the process of achieving their goals.

How your old self would see you

At certain stages in life, we have moments where we sit and ask ourselves how our younger self would see us. We could think thoughts like: How would I, five years ago, feel about me right now? He would be so disappointed in me. Well, forget about the old you for now; you're past that for a reason. The current you made certain decisions for a reason as well; respect them and respect your current self.

Your output at work

You may not always get complimented for a job well done. Most times, you just have to do your best and let everything else fall into place. You won't get any better at what you do by trying to get every colleague's opinion about your activities; it will just drive you crazy.

Whether or Not to Talk to a Loved One

It's much quicker to simply just send a text or pick up the phone and call them.

Chapter 5: How To Overcome Negativity

I can relate with people who get drained just from being on their own and in conversations with their minds. Negative thoughts have the ability to severely drain mental energy, and leave you feeling depressed, anxious, and stressed out. It might look completely harmless but trust me, it is an embodiment of all the harm you possibly know of. Name it, emotional, physical, mental, and even social harm. It sure takes a toll on your general health, even your self-esteem will not be left out.

My pain is usually expended when I meet those few guys who believe that positive thinking is a farce and that they are doing all the good they can possibly do to themself by being 'logical' and 'realistic'.

Negativity can be generated from inside-out or outside-in as the case may be. But in whatever case, none of the duo is appealing. Negativity from either of both sources have to be fought and conquered.

Below, I'll be giving succinct methods as to how to conquer each category of negativity.

How to Overcome Internally Generated Negativity

Internally generated negativity are those negativities that you feel from having a conversation with just yourself. They are your own negativity. Truth be told, this category of negativity is a harder nut to crack when compared to those generated from external forces. Let me quickly chip this in. You do not have to feel bad if you frequently feel internally generated negativity, even the most positive people wake up on the wrong side of the bed from time to time. So quit feeling bad, and let's work out a way together.

Subsequent paragraphs will be discussing the several methods through which you can deal with your own negativity:

Self-awareness is one sure way to preventing the spread of negativity to others.

It is pertinent that one first discovers the presence of a problem before one can think of providing solutions. The awareness of one's negative mental state will enable one to gain the the key to stepping out of the trap that we often get into as victims of its reactive ways.

Be in control of your emotion

Always bear in mind that emotions are fluids, they are always flowing and are hardly able to be contained,. But regardless, you are not supposed to be slave to your own emotions, you should own them. Study them so you can know how best to curtail them later in life. So instead of getting swept away by negative emotions, observe your emotional experience with curiosity.

Understand that your emotions are not stable in nature

Yes, all emotions, thoughts and feelings are fickle. They are temporary. So you do not need to beat yourself up over your emotions, you just need to observe your emotions or thoughts for a short period of time to understand their temporary nature.

Understand that this too shall pass.

Choose to Smile

By smiling, you remind yourself that you have the power to control your reactions. When you live with greater self-awareness, it's clear that how you act is always a choice.

Even if the smile feels inauthentic, still give it a try. A study published in Psychological Science showed that the physical act of smiling during stressful activities led to reduced heart rates in participants.

Ways to Overcome Externally Generated Negativity

Actively look for the good in life, nature, and the people around you

Did you notice the 'actively' in the sentence? Yea, it will most of the time not look like the best or easiest thing to do, but you have to be deliberate about it. The rule stands thus- "Seek out good things, and they will come to you." Zoom out of the negatives every once in a while. You think you are too skinny, too fall, too short, too fat, ugly, or any of those other worries that fill our minds. Take a break, smell the roses and notice the positive things around you. Trust me when I say you have to 'look for the good' this is because you actually would have to look for it.

You can actively look out for the good within your reach by any of the following and more:

Consistently savor the taste of the foods or drinks you love

Take on opportunities to learn new things, meet new people and do things that you never have.

Go for adventures.

Actively going out and look out for things you enjoy

Prioritize fun

Sometimes, all it takes to set your mood right is two hours of fun. Instead of trying to eradicate negative thoughts, get busy with having so much fun that you begin to fall in love with life all over again. Create new bucket lists of places you want to visit, foods you want to try out, and crazy things you'll like to experience. This will bring a spark of hope, and a reason to love life the more. Learn a new language, or crafts.

Be Peaceful and Smile

Always bear in mind that your interactions are an opportunity to bring others up, not tear them down, so make sure that the next time you are talking to someone, you are spreading peace and smiles. Simply being peaceful by sharing your smile is enough.

Always take a posture that takes responsibility for self

Never leave your life to chance. Phrases like "it wasn't my fault', "I had no way of knowing", "I only did that because I was stressed out", "there's nothing I could have done about this", "I had no choice", should be cut out of your statements.

Once you decide yo take charge and own your life, you'll see that you can live devoid of negative thoughts will flee. Make it clear to yourself that you're responsible for the decisions you make, you're accountable for your actions and reactions, and it's time to take control of that.

Replace Negativity

Start with your speech, make conscious efforts to kick out words that preach negativity and pessimism. Replace these words with life-giving, energy-pumping words. It is truly not a simple thing to do, but with some level of dedication and time, you will get used to it.

To fight this phenomenon called negative thoughts, be conscious of your speech and thought pattern, make sure to note the instant when these thoughts come creeping in. This is a way to fight them heads on and quickly replace them with positives.

Quit taking things personally

The truth is that quite a number of us are a pack of frustration, bitterness, anger and disappointment. You never know what someone else is going through in life. So the next time someone acts up and blows up in your face for no just cause, give them the benefit of the doubt by assuming or creating excuses for them. It could be that their loved one is sick, they just lost a job, or just anything. Most times, people's negative reaction to us have nothing to do with us. They are just expressing their negativity.

Make efforts at detaching yourself from sources of negativity

This is not a method that you can possibly go through with on a 100% scale but then, put in your best to keep negativity out. Some sources of negativity includes the social media. For me I think it is safe to say that the social media is big on initiating negative, and intimidating thoughts. Stop believing all you see on social media and trying to compare yourself with other people on the basis of what you see online. This is one big door through which negativity enters the heart of people. You are enough, and are the best version of yourself. Social media is funny in that if care is not taken, it is capable of making you envy those that you should ordinarily pity.

So the trick is if you cannot ignore the social media altogether, you could unfollow people that do great at making you feel bad about yourself.

People is another source of negativity. Some people can just decide to be in your life to just transmit all of the negative energy that they could possibly muster. And guess what? Surrounding yourself with negative people has been guaranteed to bring you down. Cut toxic people off of you and keep only those ones who are positive, supportive, and kind. And make sure that you are not sharing bad vibes or negativity into the lives of other people too. Because if you are, they will also be justified in cutting you off.

Look out for ways to glean benefits from mistakes and unpleasant occurrences.

When unpleasant events occur, ask yourself some of these questions:

What do I stand to learn from this event or occurrence?

What other way is there to doing this?

If a friend was in this situation how will I react and what will I do to help?

How would I treat a friend in this situation?

What is the positive to this narrative?

Practice positive affirmations

Always remind yourself that:

You are beautiful

You are intelligent and capable

You are strong

You are in charge, and negative thoughts have no power over you

You take positive stands in all situations

You have got the strength to overcome adverse circumstances

You react well to mistakes

You expel negativity and welcome positivity

Show acts of kindness every once in a while.

Kindness has a way of making you happy. Indeed, givers never lack, so once you are kind to people and give them reasons to be happy, happiness will not lack around you. Making others happy is a great way to make yourself more comfortable. It allows you to shift the focus off from yourself and your negative thoughts, and the positivity that will spread from your compassion will be contagious. Acts of kindness sometimes do not have to be something huge; it could be as simple as a smile at someone, or a compliment. You can be sure that as little as it is, you can brighten up someone's day with it. So henceforth, make resolves to drop kind acts here and there. Hold the door for someone or let them pass first when you're driving. Give honest and thoughtful feedback, be there for someone in need, genuinely offer to support a friend's new business, idea, or a proposition.

Be kind to yourself

This is the second twin to my earlier-mentioned point. Asides being helpful to others, you should show some kindness to yourself. Do you think you are kind to yourself? Well, if you cannot say what you're thinking of yourself to your best friend, then you're unnecessarily cruel to yourself. Treat yourself like you would a dear friend, with all the patience and compassion that is required.

Give yourself breaks, indulge yourself sometimes. Of course you will have bad days, don't lash out. Quit pushing yourself hard. Reward yourself and treat yourself to some luxurious getaways sometimes. You're not going to be perfect, and that's part of your beauty. Take it easy and be kind. You deserve to be treated with compassion, especially from yourself.

Chapter 6: Types Of Overthinking

Overthinking is a point of view that is excessively mind boggling bringing about sat around idly, chance because of inaction and low-quality choices.

Thinking about an excessive number of variables in a choice without separating and gauging significance.

Blaming the basic leadership process so as to abstain from something you would prefer not to do.

Disregarding something you definitely know.

Sitting around idly and assets pondering a choice that shouldn't be made at this point.

Seeing issues where they don't exist.

Slowing down on a choice because of missing data.

You wind up making each circumstance in your life about 100x more difficult than it must be.

You can't release anything since you're persuaded that if you simply keep running over the subtleties a couple of more occasions, you'll at long last reveal some new comprehension of the circumstance or it will some way or another change the result.

You've most likely never been secure with a thing in your life. You've drawn nearer everything from picking a school and an accomplice to your outfit toward the beginning of the day and brand of bread at the market with equivalent degrees of tension.

You're always saying thanks to the companions who stick around to hear you think about similar subtleties of a circumstance or relationship over and over, and however you never truly land at a different end, only the demonstration of overthinking is sufficient for you.

Rest is the most difficult part of your life since laying quietly in obscurity is the main time you aren't diverted enough to not have the option to sink into dashing considerations.

If somebody ever parts ways with you/decays to go out with you, you persuade yourself this is a direct result of a hundred irrelevant stumbles you made.

You wind up tormenting yourself over each other worn-out side remark somebody makes in light of the fact that clearly there is some significance to be revealed, it's unmistakably simply an issue of considering it until you discover it.

Chapter 7: How To Overcome

Procrastination Step By Step

Assume that is Monday afternoon, and the time is passing by. You are finishing up all your works furiously for submitting the same before 5'o clock, which is your deadline. At the same time, you are also cursing yourself for the reason for not starting the work on time. But how did this happen? What is the thing which went wrong? What made you lose your focus from work? Well, the reason is the hours of the day which you spent in scrolling down your social media, re-reading all your mails, taking longer coffee breaks, and also the time which you spend on those tasks which could have been easily done after a few days. All of these happen because of procrastination.

Procrastination can be regarded as a trap in your way to success. It is nothing but the practice of doing the less urgent types of works with more preference in place of the ones on which you should actually work. It results in the delay of the important tasks and thus often resulting in failure.

Is procrastination and laziness the same thing?

Procrastination is often compared with being lazy, but in actual they are two different things. Procrastination is an active kind of process in which you can choose to do some other kind of work in place of the one which you know should be done. Unlike procrastination, laziness comes along with inactivity, apathy, and also unwillingness for acting in the desired way. Procrastination generally involves ignoring those tasks which are unpleasant but are also important in nature in favor of those tasks, which is much more easier or enjoyable.

When you give in easily to the impulses of procrastination, it might provide you with some serious form of consequences. For instance, even the slightest incidents of procrastination can make you feel ashamed or even guilty. It can also result in a reduced degree of productivity and can also cause you to easily miss out all your achieving goals. When you keep on procrastinating for a long time, you are most likely to become disillusioned and also demotivated with all your important works, which can also eventually result in depression and even joblessness when it goes out of hand.

How can you cope up with procrastination?

As with most of your habits, it is actually possible for us to deal with procrastination. You can follow the mentioned steps below for dealing with and for preventing procrastination.

Recognizing that you are actually procrastinating: You might have the tendency of putting off any task as you need to re-prioritize the workload that you have. If you are knowingly delaying a task which is important in nature for an actual good kind of reason, you are not at all procrastinating then. But, in case you start to put the tasks off in an indefinite manner or just simply switch your focus every now and then as all that you want is to avoid a particular thing, then you are most likely to procrastinate. You might also find yourself procrastinating in case you:

Try to fill up your whole day with tasks that are of less or no priority in actual.

Leaving any item on your list for a very long time even when you know that it is important for you.

Reading all your emails many times without even taking any form of decision on what you are required to do with all of them.

Starting with a task of high priority and then taking a long break for no reason at all.

Filling up your routine with the tasks of other people instead of the ones which are important for you to get them done on time.

Waiting for the perfect mood or for the perfect time always for tackling any tough task.

Working on the reason why you are probably procrastinating: You are required to understand the very reasons why you are actually procrastinating right before you start with the processes of tackling it. For example, are you having the tendency to avoid some particular sort of tasks as you are finding them unpleasant or boring in nature? If that is the case, you need to take your steps out of the same very quickly so that it becomes possible for you to easily focus on each and every aspect of the tasks so that you can find them more enjoyable. Poor form of organization can also result in procrastination. People who are of organized nature can easily overcome the traits of procrastination as they are of the habit of using a prioritized form of to-do-lists and can also create an effective form of schedules. Such tools can help in organizing all the tasks by deadline and priority.

It might happen that even if you are organized in nature, you might get overwhelmed by any task. In case you have any doubt on your very own ability and you are also worried about the thought of failing, you are required to put off that particular task and find out for comfort in some other kind of work which you know you have the capability of completing on time and perfectly. There are various people who have a fear of success, exactly like the fear of failure. Such people have the tendency to think that success will make them filled up with more requests by others for taking some more work. But, surprisingly, the people who are actually perfectionists by nature are also procrastinators. Such people would often avoid doing any kind of task which they feel incapable of doing and would rather on the tasks which they could pull off perfectly.

Another cause related to procrastination is poor form of decision making. In case you are not even able to decide what you should be doing, you are most likely to decide to take up the wrong action and finish the thing in the wrong way. For many people, procrastination might even turn out to be more than just a mere bad habit. It might also be a sign of an underlying issue of health. For instance, anxiety, depression, OCD, and ADHD are also linked along with procrastination.

It has also been found from various studies that it might also be the cause of any serious form of illness and stress. So, in case you are also suffering from this debilitating or chronic form of procrastination, you can blame these many reasons, and it is high time for you to start with the process of coping up with the same.

Adopting various strategies of anti-procrastination: Procrastination is often referred to as a habit, which is a kind of behavior of deeply ingrained patterns. In simple words, you will not be able to break its spell overnight. You can stop your habits from being the habits by avoiding practicing them and so you are required to take up any of the strategies mentioned below for succeeding from the grip of procrastination.

You can start by forgiving yourself for procrastinating in the earlier days. It has been found that self-forgiveness comes with the power of making you feel much more positive than usual regarding yourself, and it can also help in reducing the chances of procrastination in the upcoming days.

You can prevent procrastination by committing to the tasks. You are required to focus on doing the tasks and not just avoiding them indefinitely. You can do this by simply writing down all the jobs that you are required to finish and also specify a time frame for the same. This will be helping you in tackling your works in a proactive way.

You can also ask someone else to continuously check on you. It is true that peer pressure actually works. This is the prime principle on which the self-help groups rely on. You can also opt for self-monitoring in case you have no one to check up on you.

You need to act up as you go. Tackling all the tasks as soon as you receive them instead of just piling them up can help a lot.

You can rephrase the dialog of your inner-self. Various phrases such as 'have to' and 'need to,' for instance, helps in implying that you are left with no other choice in doing what you are supposed to do. This might even result in making you feel disempowered and can also result in cases of self-sabotage. But, when you use phrases such as 'I choose to,' it helps in implying that you are owning a project, and it can also make you feel having control of the entire workload that you have.

Minimizing all your distractions is of prime importance. Try to turn off your social media along with your email and also avoid sitting in a place that is close to the television for your work.

Try to do all those tasks which you do not like in the first hour of the day. This will help in making you feel more concentrated on doing the tasks which you love.

Tip: There is also an alternative form of approach which embraces the subtle art of delaying. According to various researches, an active form of procrastination which is delaying all your tasks deliberately so that you can give your focus in doing the urgent jobs can help in making you feel much more challenged along with motivated for getting all the things done on time. This approach works specifically if you are the kind of person who actually thrives under extreme pressure.

In case you are procrastinating as you are finding a particular task very unpleasant or boring, you are required to actually focus on the long form of the game. It has been found from various studies that people who are of impulsive nature are most likely to procrastinate as all that they are focused on are the short-term gains. You are required to fight against this by recognizing the long-term gains or benefits after you complete the entire task. Another effective way of making your work feel more enjoyable is by identifying all the unpleasant form of consequences for avoiding the same. For example, imagine situations that what is going to happen in case you do not complete the task? How is the situation going to affect you personally, your team, or even organizational form of goals?

In case you procrastinate only because you are disorganized by nature, follow these tips, which can turn you into an organized person.

Try to create a to-do list. This helps in preventing forgetting all your tasks, which are unpleasant in nature.

You can try to prioritize some of the specific tasks in your to-do list. It helps in the identification of all those tasks which you should actually focus on along with the ones which you can actually ignore.

Try to use the method of scheduling and planning. When you are having a big-sized project or various projects at one time, and you are not aware of the point from where you should start, you can try out planning and scheduling which also helps in using up all your time in the most effective way and also helps in relieving your stress.

Try to tackle all the tough jobs at your preferred peak time. Do you work your best in the afternoon or early in the morning? Try to find out your most effective time so that you can finish all the hard tasks within that period of time.

Set up goals that are bounded by time. When you set up particular deadlines for completing all your tasks, you can easily be on track for achieving all your goals, and thus, you will be left with no time for procrastination.

You can try out various applications for the management of your tasks. If you are unable to plan out your schedule, such tools can help you in planning properly.

If you are very much prone to delaying all the projects as you find them overwhelming, you can try to break them in small and manageable forms of chunks. You can easily organize your schedule when you have small chunks of tasks to be completed, and you will also find it a lot easier to start with them.

Taking a break: It is important for you to give your mind a break of 10-15 minutes whenever your work timer gets off. Try to listen to music, read books, or take a short walk in that period of time. It will help your mind to concentrate on the hard task again and will also make you feel more motivated than before. When you work on constantly without taking any kind of break, your brain is very likely to get overworked and ultimately results in getting blocked with all your works. Try to give your mind the space it needs for breathing, and after you return t0 work from a short break, you can easily find out the difference in your confidence and concentration, and thus, you will be able to finish off with your work quickly and also in the perfect way.

Getting rid of catastrophizing: One of the very reasons why people procrastinate is because they tend to make a large deal out of a very small thing or simply catastrophize. You are most likely to catastrophize when you feel stressed with work or feel bored in completing the task. So, when you stop catastrophizing, you can easily get your work done like all the tasks which you love without any signs of procrastination.

Being realistic: Fooling yourself by acting that a particular task won't take much time is not the ideal thing to do. Try being as much realistic as you can. Don't just provide yourself with up to the mark time. Try to bake in some extra time so that you can finish the work peacefully. When you hurry with any job, you are most likely to procrastinate as you might feel stressed or anxious about the work. Giving your job a little extra time will provide you with the peace of mind which you need to get your job done on time.

Rewarding yourself: Who doesn't love rewards? Right? Try to set up rewards for your very self as you finish up your work on time. If you love being on social platforms, try to set the same as your reward, which you are not going to use unless and until you finish off with your work. It will also provide you with the motivation that you need.

Chapter 8: Stress And Stress Management

In everyday use, stress can be defined as a feeling which people have when they become overloaded and struggle to handle demands. Oftentimes, these demands are associated with their occupation, money, or relationship, among other situations. However, anything which serves as a real or observed threat or challenge to the well-being of a person is capable of leading to stress. When it is, stress can be motivational, especially in times when survival is of the highest import. The flight-or-fight response informs us when and how to react in times of danger. However, if the response is easily triggered, or when too many stressors act together at the same time, it can put the physical and mental well-being of a person at risk. Based on the stress survey carried out annually by the APA (American Psychological Association), the average stress levels of people in the United States has grown from 4.9 to 5.1 on a scale of 1 to 10 in 2015. The main reasons for the growing stress rates were attributed to money and employment.

Key Facts About Stress

Below are some major facts you should know about stress so as to be able to manage and combat it.

Stress is a helpful response which primes the body to respond to danger.

The signs and symptoms of stress can be experienced both psychologically and physically.

Short-term stress is helpful when it is short, but long-term stress has been traced to several health risks.

Self-management hacks can help you prepare for and manage stress.

From a biological perspective, stress can be seen as the natural defense of the body against danger. Stress clears the body system using hormones to prep the body to avoid or combat attacks. As was mentioned earlier, this response is called the flight-or-fight mechanism. When challenges come our way, some part of our response is largely physical. As a response, the body activates certain resources which defend and prepare it either to remain and fight or flee from the danger as quickly as possible.

The body produces chemicals such as noradrenaline, adrenaline, and cortisol in large quantities. These chemicals trigger heightened senses, preparedness in the muscles, alertness, increased heart rate, and sweating. All these elements increase our ability to react to a dangerous and challenging happening. The environmental factors which result in these reactions are known as stressors. Some of them are aggressive behavior, speeding cars, horrific moments in films, a first-time outing, loud, unexpected noises, etc. The more stressors we are exposed to, the more stress the body builds up.

The Effects of Stress on the Body

Below are some of the effects stress has on the body:

increased pulse rate and rise in blood pressure

increased rate of breathing

decrease in activity of the digestive system

tension in the muscles

a heightened sense of alertness which causes sleeplessness

Types of Stress

According to the American Psychological Association, there are three distinct types of stress which require various levels of stress management.

1. Acute stress:

Acute stress is a type of stress which occurs in the short term. It is the most common type of stress there is. Acute stress is usually triggered by overthinking the pressure caused by events which have happened in recent times. Acute stress could also occur as a result of upcoming demands in the future.

If, for instance, you have been in an argument lately which has made you upset or you have a daunting task that is quickly approaching, you could have experienced stress triggers. Oftentimes, the resolution of these things you find daunting will not only be less scary than you thought but will sometimes quell your stress altogether. Acute stress doesn't result in much damage like chronic or long-term stress can. Short-term effects of acute stress include stomach upsets, distress, anxiety, and tension headaches. However, repetitive cases of acute stress across an extended period can lead to chronic stress and become more harmful.

2. Episodic acute stress:

If you experience acute stress frequently or are constantly surrounded by periodic stress triggers, you are at risk of having episodic acute stress. Episodic stress is usually triggered by being overwhelmed and having a poor sense of organization. Thus, factors like a heightened sense of irritation and tension are symptoms of episodic acute stress building up in the body. These elements can cause one to resort to worrying and overthinking, making you more stressed. In worse case scenarios, episodic acute stress can lead to heart conditions and high blood pressure.

3. Chronic stress:

Chronic stress is arguably the most harmful type of stress there is, the reason being that it lingers for a long time. Triggers such as overthinking, being overwhelmed, sadness, etc., can lead to chronic stress. It usually occurs when you feel that there is no way of escape from your fears and give up on the possibility of any solution whatsoever. Chronic stress can also be as a result of traumatic or scarring experiences. Unlike other forms of stress which are noticeable and easily managed, chronic stress can exist unnoticed, especially when it becomes habitual in a person. In doing this, it forms a part of the person's identity, making them susceptible to the effects of stress without regards to the events they may face. If you have chronic stress, chances are high that you could have a breakdown, physically and mentally. Chronic stress can put you at risk of suicidal behavior, violent breakdowns, strokes, and heart conditions, among others.

How to Manage Stress

Below are a few steps with which you can manage your stress levels and prevent feelings of being overwhelmed and other devastating effects:

1. Exercise regularly:

It has been proven that working out is beneficial in improving the physical and mental state of the human body. Thus, exercising can help reduce stress levels in the body.

2. Reduce your intake of drugs like caffeine and alcohol:

Drugs like caffeine and alcohol are not substances that help you cope with or prevent stress. If anything, they tend to worsen it, so cut down on your intake or refrain from it totally.

3. Good nutrition:

Eating a good, healthy, and balanced meal can help you cope with stress. Foods like veggies and fruits help keep the immune system at an optimal level. Poor diets will do you no good and only result in poor health and more stress.

4. Set your priorities right:

Take the time out to organize your life and plan your time. Set up a to-do list about the important stuff, then focus on completing them. This will help you have a fulfilled day and keep you from worrying or overthinking about the things you have yet to achieve.

5. Manage your time:

Take the time out each day to just cut back and relax. Spend some time with yourself, in which you get your ducks in a row and recharge for the pursuits of your goals. Simply destress.

6. Relax and breathe:

Sometimes, spend some time doing yoga, meditation, and massage. You can also use relaxation and breathing techniques to slow down the body's systems and help you destress.

7. Try talking:

Talking to people like your friends, colleagues, and family can also help you cope with stress. Baring your worries to people you feel close to can help reduce the strain of worry and overthinking, putting you in a better frame of mind to function better. In this state, you may find that there are better ways of approaching your concerns.

8. Pay attention to symptoms:

Sometimes, you may get so worked up worrying and stressing yourself out that you may not notice the effects the problem is having on you. Learn to control your stress levels by being attentive to signs and symptoms. When you notice you are becoming stressed, it is time to cut back. The first and best course of action is to notice that you are stressed. If you are stressed because of being overwhelmed from work or negative thinking, then perhaps it is time you stopped and just breathe. You can also consider lowering your workload in the case of being overwhelmed from work and being more mindful in the case of overthinking and worrying.

9. Find the destressor that works for you:

Everybody has that one thing that seems to help them relax. For some, it might be listening to music. Others might find reading relaxing, while others could also go on a walk, work out, speak to friends, play games, or sing or play with their pet.

10. Find and join a support network:

According to the American Psychological Association, it is advisable to become a part of a network of social support. For instance, you could talk to your neighbors and other people in your locale, join a local club or charity group, or become a part of a religious organization. Even if you don't exactly feel stressed now, joining a group can prevent the occurrence of stress, and provide psychological and emotional support in times of need. Joining an online social network can also be a helpful alternative; however, make sure that it doesn't replace physical networking. Online networking can be especially helpful in contacting people not close to you and can aid in lowering the risk of stress and anxiety.

Chapter 9: Gain Control Over Worry

Stress is the relentless negative considerations that recurrent themselves. You can deal with your considerations. These contemplations trick you into accepting that you thin since they are musings about issues. In any case, each time you "think" about the issue, similar musings repeat. These considerations never take care of the issue, nor do they advance your circumstance in any capacity. Stress pursues an example:

•Your musings rehash what you definitely think about the circumstance by portraying what occurred or characterizing the issue

•You assemble proof to safeguard your inclination by discovering other negative articulations from encounters throughout your life to fabricate a case to help the end you have come to or the passionate position you have taken.

•You feel legitimized in having sentiments, for example, fault or disdain on account of the circumstance. You may really be pleased with being exploited by this circumstance and safeguard it.

Exercise to Break Through Worry

The initial step is to tune in to what your mind lets you know. This is designated "self-talk". Convey a scratch pad and pencil and record it for a couple of days. Request that your watchman heavenly attendant assistance you have the mental fortitude to see this piece of yourself plainly:

Dear Guardian Angel, help me to end up mindful of the negative musings controlling my psyche. Encourage me to deal with my contemplations and quit stressing so I can discover genuine arrangements.

The following are a couple of my genuine contemplations that I recorded when I was caught in stress:

I'm continually thinking, however my position never shows signs of change. My circumstance is unthinkable. For what reason do I settle on such awful decisions? There must be some kind of problem with me. I am such a trick. For what reason do I tune in to individuals who lie to me? I am biting the dust of dejection. For what reason am I so alone? I feel so lost. I loathe my life. Everything is a battle. For what reason does everything need to be so difficult? I continue scanning for answers that never come. I've committed such a large number of errors. I don't have anybody near to converse with. I feel miserable.

There is trust. It takes assurance and constancy to change negative considerations propensities. Stress is alluring on the grounds that there is in every case a trace of validity in it. The mind turns that small trace of legitimacy into an entire situation of disappointment. Take a gander at the sentences you have caught utilizing the accompanying four stages and my case of self-talk:

Stage 1: Find the trace of legitimacy. "I'm continually thinking, yet my position never shows signs of change." Both pieces of that are valid.

Stage 2: What emotions does it trigger? I feel idiotic that I settle on awful choices. I feel miserable, lost, and alone. I am disappointed that nothing changes. I am furious with God for not giving me what I need. I censure others for my terrible circumstances. I feel furious that nobody is safeguarding me.

Stage 3: How would you sum up? "I'm continually thinking" is a general proclamation. When you discover the speculation, ask yourself inquiries like: Am I scanning for inquiries concerning explicit pieces of my circumstance and after that looking for answers? Am I attempting to discover individuals who are reliable and could help with my circumstances? Or on the other hand, am I rehashing negative musings about past occasions and calling that reasoning? "My position never shows signs of change." This is another speculation. Quest for some fact: There must be some little change that occurs. I could hope to see explicitly what has changed.

Stage 4: Think of 5 moves you can make to change.

(1) My feelings are a powder barrel. I could ride the activity bicycle each morning for 15 minutes and discharge the sentiments in the power of accelerating. At that point, I can begin the day in an open and responsive state.

(2) I could contact a companion who could bolster me in rolling out positive improvement.

(3) I could consider my circumstance and separate it into pieces.

(4) Then I could concentrate on the most significant piece first.

(5) I could make that rundown of things that have changed in my life as motivation

and continue adding to it as new changes happen.

Give up and Move On

After you have analyzed the substance of what you are agonizing over and discovered accommodating activities, let it go. Choose to quit stressing. The giving up beginnings as a craving in your heart and turns into a move in your disposition. Close your eyes and envision how extraordinary you would feel inside yourself if your heart were available to feel love. While you will most likely be unable to change your conditions for quite a while, how might your life change on the off chance that you concentrated on positive, gainful contemplations?

Concentrate on a greater picture to discover an enduring change. What does God need for you? He needs you to go to Him with your agony. God needs you to look for His adoration to fill your desolate, hurting heart. He needs to comfort you and help you to discover mending. He needs to control you through troublesome changes to discover more truth and opportunity. He needs you to look for His methods of adoration. Be serious and careful about this change. Each time you discover yourself stressing, recall the master plan of your craving for adoration and call to your gatekeeper holy messenger for assistance. Your undertaking is bringing change. Push ahead and don't think back.

POSITIVE THINKING AND OVERCOMING NEGATIVITY

Negative contemplations are the best deterrent on the planet. Somebody who is experiencing interminable negativity lacks the opportunity to expand their potential throughout everyday life. Conquering negativity is important to complete any errand. At the point when contrary musings are permitted to thrive, the individual tainted will have next to no opportunity of encountering development and achievement. Consistently we are shelled with data and along these lines, fear, anxiety and stress can enter our brain without much of stress. Negativity is a fight inside yourself. Nobody can remove this issue except if you are focused on conquering negativity.

Expelling anxiety, uncertainty and fear isn't a simple errand: it will include a procedure. It will involve you concentrating on positive reasoning. Indeed, even in the most critical circumstances, something positive can come up yet it takes readiness, inventiveness and attention to perceive what are these issues can be transformed into something helpful.

Negative contemplations can be life depleting. They can lead an individual to question themselves and not follow up on their fantasies. For instance, such a large number of individuals stall out on making road challenges, however neglect to think of elective answers for the issue. While dissenting in the city is anything but a poorly conceived notion in the event that you need to make others mindful, it ought to be combined with positive activities that can tap the enthusiasm of others.

Positive reasoning is the capacity to make and to motivate. It isn't just about changing your considerations; however, ensuring that it means activities in your everyday life generally the positive contemplations won't give the effect that you might want to have.

So as to prepare yourself to have a superior outlook, it is ideal to figure out how to quiet down your considerations down. It's simpler to make positive musings if your considerations are masterminded in such a way, that you can control them. Notwithstanding when life gets excessively occupied and wild set aside the effort to inhale gradually, unwind and void your musings through contemplation.

Contemplation is the specialty of not considering anything or simply concentrating on pondering pictures that you might want to occur. The psyche can be prepared to see a greatly improved point of view, for instance even an individual in prison can traverse the hardest days by figuring out how to think decidedly, they can envision the stream banks, the daylight, the woodland and other attractive characteristics of nature like roses as opposed to concentrating on their predicament.

As a rule, individuals are able to remain engaged, quiet and can keep up positive musings. Empowering others in spite of the conditions is do-plausible. However, so as to get to positive reasoning, you have to figure out how to teach your psyche so as to beat negativity.

Positive reasoning is for the most part about contemplating right now and not agonizing over the subtleties of the past and what's to come. It is tied in with preparing the psyche and body to react to what they can change now, not what they want almost certainly work upon because of different conditions. It is tied in with being alert and benefiting as much as possible from a given circumstance.

HOW TO OVERCOME NEGATIVE THOUGHTS AND EMOTIONS

So far we have arranged the dirt, picked which seed to plant (objective); and planted the seed. What's left to do is to sustain the seed and ensure it leaves the ground effectively. Also, when it's out, we need to protect the youthful plant in its condition to ensure its life isn't snuffed out before it arrives at a phase where we can gladly harvest its delectable natural products.

To begin with, the seed will have its very own fundamental obstacles to surmount, for example, advancing around stones in the dirt, etc. When it figures out how to demonstrate its head as a seedling, you should be cautious its development isn't defeated by weeds, slugs and different irritations.

I surmise you can see where I am going with this. It's conceivable to compare the vermin and weed to the wide scope of negative contemplations and sentiments you need to attempt to control after the Prayer Ritual.

Contemplations and emotions are substances and will pull in comparable conditions and individuals into your life. Pessimistic musings and emotions you realize will pull in unfavorable conditions and individuals who will obstruct you from achieving the objective you have set forward.

On the off chance that you are going have the option to trim in these wellsprings of negative vibrational frequencies, you have to see how they are interconnected.

An idea makes a sentiment of a comparative sort. This idea and feeling will direct the move you make. Redundancy of this idea and feel will bring about the rehashed activity which will add up to a propensity. In the event that the first idea was negative, this propensity would be negative. The negative propensity, as is not out of the ordinary, will induce undesirable conditions or results throughout your life. The negative outcomes will at that point create related negative convictions. The last will bring forth a negative idea. On the off chance that fitting advances are not taken to capture the brokenness, this negative cycle will turn into the request for the day. The accompanying outline ought to represent this piece:

You have a set an 'objective sum' that is about twice your present compensation. You have been propelled to go for another activity in Public Relations that will pay you a compensation somewhat over your 'objective sum'. You are shortlisted and have been brought in for a meeting. Toward the beginning of the day as you excitedly remain before the mirror sprucing up, an inward exchange results. A voice inside your head starts to connect with you an awful chat.

"Wow take a gander at the size of your head", it says. Before you could reply back it includes,

"what's more, it's a major head as well as it is uncovered and dark." You figure out how to reply back with something like, "My head isn't huge."

This internal voice won't shut up, and it proceeds to state: "Ah Pareto proportion! Your nose is multiple times as large as that of every other person, and this should be a PR talk with; looks matter!" You do your best to quiet this inward voice, without any result. It is practically winning the fight as you are getting dampened. Does this example of negative internal talk sound well-known? Nearly everyone is a casualty of it. That is the place question, stress, anxiety and a great deal of stress come from.

You get so worked up in the event that you could physically haul out that voice you would give it a whack on the head and request that it "zip it"! You could be as intended to it as this person was to his parrot.

The person purchased a talking parrot and took him home. The parrot talked and talked. The issue was he swore constantly. It was humiliating. The man took a stab at everything: he beseeched him and he compromised him. Nothing worked.

At last, he decided that remarkable measures would be required. He cautioned the parrot that he was going to place him in the cooler in the event that he didn't quiet down its bill. The winged creature continued swearing, so he got him by the neck, tossed him in the cooler, and after that pummeled the entryway.

Following 60 minutes, he opened the cooler way to discover a nearly solidified parrot. The man asked, "Presently, would you say you are going to quit swearing?" Appalled by the experience, the parrot stated, "Truly, I'll never swear again." Then motioning toward the cooler, he asked, "Yet one inquiry: What the damnation did that chicken do?"

In an endeavor to conquer antagonistic thoughts, many individuals will in general restrict the negative idea rationally by utilizing words like 'not', 'don't, etc. As I referenced in a prior exercise, the intuitive personality does not enlist words, for example, 'don't, and 'not'. This kind of resistance strategy bothers the circumstance.

An extremely compelling system that is utilized to beat negative thoughts and sentiments is to rehash a positive assertion that makes the negative idea false and frail. How about we take a gander at certain models. To a negative idea, for example, "I am too worn out to even consider doing this work". You could state something like: "When I start this work, and my consideration is retained, it will turn out to be progressively simpler". Or on the other hand even a straightforward sentence, for example, "I am solid and capable" rehashed a couple of times, will dissipate the negative idea.

Actually the shorter the positive certification, the better. Single positive words can be extremely incredible. Simply rehashing words, for example, harmony, happiness or love to yourself can work. Another method that can be entirely dependable in expelling negative thoughts and emotions is an authentic expansive grin. A couple of them can improve your whole state of mind and your thoughts will go with the same pattern.

Once in awhile it utilizes your legitimate personality to truly persuade yourself that the antagonistic thoughts are outlandish and false. This kind of pondering will assist you in generating the most intense positive attestation. For instance, on the off chance that you discover yourself thinking: "This money related objective is excessively high, I can't accomplish it." Look around and endeavor to make sense of the number of individuals who have accomplished what you are going for. You would then be able to think of confirmation like: "Numerous individuals have accomplished this. I am capable; yes I can!" Focus your every consideration on the positive assertion and articulate it a few times, and the negative idea and its related inclination will evaporate immediately and inexplicably.

At the point when things get downright awful, and you are attempting to think of a positive certification to ward off the negative, there is another method. It is the thing that I for one term the system of 'Toning it down would be ideal'. The idea is in a state of harmony with an adage from the Ashanti clan in Ghana that truly deciphers: "On the off chance that you are wearing clothes, you don't play battle". Consider it. On the off chance that your shirt is as of now self-destructing on you, and somebody gets it, you would instinctively stop, and simply trust that individual will be benevolent enough to relinquish it. More often than not he would. In the event that you attempt to move while your shirt is being held, you would wind up with an uncovered middle! Simply remain as quiet as you can and watch your negative idea as it travels every which way. Try not to get genuinely joined to them. You accomplish this by mentally disconnecting yourself from the passing thoughts. Become an eyewitness and simply watch them go, with the conviction that they are simply short-lived thoughts. What's more, they would be. It fills in as though the negative thoughts become disheartened on the grounds that they realize they are not having the proposed effect on you. They evaporate a great deal sooner than they had proposed to remain. In these times of perception, you can likewise detect your most bothering negative thoughts, and make some positive assertions ahead of time to disperse them next time they appear.

I can't wrap this dialog up without sharing a strategy that has worked for me as a matter of course. It's extremely straightforward. Dig into your life and search for the scarcest thing you can be grateful for. Furthermore, start to wholeheartedly thank the Universe, God, the Great Spirit, etc. Show earnest appreciation for the positive qualities throughout your life. Trust me, negative thoughts and feelings detest this training with enthusiasm. They will escape without saying goodbye to you.

Anxiety is an infection that will push your objective extremely distant from you. Be vigilant for it, when your objective seems deferred. Once in a while, you would be that near your objective; don't give anxiety a chance to set in. Anxiety can be compared to a rodent that continues burrowing around the seed you planted to make sense of when it would create natural products. It truly would stunt the advancement of the seed (your objective).

119

ADVICE ON OVERCOMING NEGATIVE THOUGHTS

Our psyches are continually besieged with defeating negative thoughts whether intentionally or intuitively. Be that as it may, we must be responsible for how we react to conquering negative thoughts and this is the place the arrangement lies.

You can assume responsibility for your thoughts and feelings or enable them to assume responsibility for you.

At the point when an idea comes into your psyche, be it positive or negative, you can dispense with it or harp on it: you have that decision. In any case, the more you harp on negative thoughts the quicker you slip by into a condition of anxiety and sorrow.

The pessimistic individual will in general have a self-focused and repulsive mentality towards life estranging themselves. They accuse their setback of every other person though the responsibility lies exclusively with them.

They think and will themselves into coming up short at all that they attempt to accomplish through the constructive individual may bomb in some cases yet will take in a significant exercise from disappointment and will react as needs are.

You will find that there is a positive side to everything. It is an instance of attempting to recognize it and react each time a negative idea comes into your brain. At that point, you should dispose of it and supplant it with a positive idea. A few people locate this difficulty yet by concentrating on all that is great in your life and all that you must be grateful for constructive reasoning ends up simpler.

It is that Mother Nature gives us a lot to be grateful for. You just need to check out your surroundings to value the excellence and miracle of everything.

Focusing on all that is great in your life places negativity in context. In time your negative thoughts become less and less.

Accordingly you are continuously conquering negative thoughts.

In spite of the fact that your mind will in any case be barraged with negative thoughts, on the off chance that you expel them while staying positive, your mentality will improve as will your personal satisfaction.

Imprint has focused on this matter as in his youth he was scourged by the absence of self-certainty and low self-regard and might want to share his encounters of how he has beaten these issues with the expectation that it will help other people vanquish comparable issues.

Chapter 10: How To Overcome Worry,

Fear, Anxiety, And Other Obstacles

Have you ever tried to take a step forward but you find yourself going back to where you started? Or sometimes, end up not taking a step because you are worried or scared of what the outcome could be? Try asking yourself why and see if you can come up with any valid reasons. It might just be a negative thought, as we discussed in the previous chapter.

We are aware that fear can create strong response signals, especially during emergencies; it is one of the most powerful emotions and gets away with playing tricks on your mind and body. You find fear in almost every aspect of your life, even during situations that do not warrant fear like examinations, a date, a party, even a new job. It is a natural response to threats that the mind can perceive.

Anxiety, on the other hand, refers to certain types of fear that have to do with the thought of a threat, a negative thought to be precise, that you perceive to occur in the future - it doesn't focus on the present. These two, fear and anxiety, can either last for a short period or can last even longer and linger in your mind. Fear is capable of taking over your sanity; sleeping and eating will become difficult and you cannot enjoy any moment of life without having to worry about something. This can hold you back from doing things you want or need to do, and if it continues on, health is affected, especially mental health.

There are some people who are overwhelmed by fear and avoid situations that make them experience fear. For example, when someone starts dating a new partner, they could be scared of commitment and after a break up because of this reason, may decide not to want to get into a relationship again. The person may not be able to break this cycle but at a point, they could decide to face this fear and learn to feel less fearful and to cope with the fear. They chose to work on themselves and took their fear head-on. You can also learn to feel the same way, to cope with fear so that it won't take away the interesting and fun aspects of your life. Worry is another obstacle that we tend to face, it is normal to be worried about things, but it becomes a serious obstacle when it is persistent and uncontrollable. When we talked about limiting beliefs and negative thoughts, we pointed out "what ifs" - this is where those thoughts are being formed about potential happenings.

Worries leave you with many things to deal with, and even unnecessary ones like an upset stomach, muscle tension, fidgeting, restlessness, and can even cause insomnia, which will show in your performance in school or even at work. You can even form habits out of being worried; habits like excessive alcohol consumption, drug abuse, and you may even take out your negative feelings on people around you, you find people who are so worried to the point that they begin to zone out during a conversation or even while staring at a screen. Chronic worrying is also a major symptom of Generalized Anxiety Disorder (GAD) – a common anxiety disorder that colors your whole life, leaving you constantly nervous, tensed, and with a general feeling of unease.

How to Overcome These Obstacles

Face your fears

Remember the example stated about being scared of commitments? If you are constantly avoiding situations that scare you, you might end up not doing things that you need to do, so there will be no opportunity to see if the situation is as bad as you expect it to be. Hence, miss out on the opportunity to devise a means of managing your fear. It is also advisable that you write down what those worries or fears are - set a time to do that as an activity and think about each of the worries; put them in black and white and then try to continue your day without having to think about them again. It is almost like creating a worry period where you allow yourself to tackle these fears or worries and create a balanced perspective. You might be surprised that you find out you're bothered about something that adds no value to you.

Exercise

You should make time to exercise. Exercise requires concentration and when you're making an effort to concentrate on the activities of your exercise, you tend to take your mind off your fears and worries. You definitely can't be playing soccer and still be wondering if your job application is going to be successful or not. Your exercise time is a relaxation period and when you make this a habit, the better you become at handling your obstacle.

Distinguish between solvable and unsolvable worries

Dividing your worries and fears into two groups: solvable and unsolvable. Let's assume you are worried about an upcoming examination, your mother's health issues, and your country's economic recession. Looking at these three worries, you can see that the outcome of your upcoming examination is in your hands if you want a good grade. You need to prepare well ahead of the exam in order to have it under your control. Your mother's health is not in my control, you are not a medical doctor, and at the same time, you don't have the solution to the problem. Leave it to the experts in that field. Lastly, your country's economic recession is a worry that is beyond you, it's something you have no control over, nothing you say or do can change the situation.

If you can't change the situation, then why worry? And if you can change it, why worry?

Talking therapies

Counseling or cognitive behavioral therapy are good examples of talking therapies and are very effective for people with anxiety. It may seem like a simple solution but talking to a therapist is usually effective and they can offer methods to use in overcoming these fears or worries.

Talk about your worries

This is another simple solution that involves talking face-to-face with someone you trust. It might be your friend or family member, anyone who would listen to you and not judge or criticize you or get distracted when listening. It is one of the most effective ways to calm yourself down and relieve anxiety or worry in you. When you begin to talk about your worries, they start to feel less threatening. Keeping them to yourself will only create build-up and then it may start to scare you. If your fears are unwarranted, verbalizing them can reveal them for what they are. Even if these fears are things you should be scared of, talking to someone and sharing this with someone can bring about a solution that you may have not been able to think or come up with alone.

Build a strong support system

We are social creatures - we feel the need to socialize, to be around people, we don't always want to live in isolation, although, we like to enjoy your peace and privacy at certain times. A strong support system doesn't have to be a wide network of friends. There is a strong benefit in having people around you who you can trust and count on at any given time. Never underestimate the power of friendship, and if you feel you do not have anyone, it is not too late to start building new friendships. You don't have to go out there looking desperately for friendships, just take it as it comes.

Practice mindfulness

Worrying is always focused on events that are yet to happen or on past events. They might not even happen, but yet you're still bothered about if it were to happen, or, with the past, it could be rethinking things you said to someone, actions you took which you feel you shouldn't have or could have done better. Mindfulness practice can help you to break away from worries or fears of yours by shifting your attention back to what is happening in the present. This is not a new practice; it has been around for centuries. This practice allows you to observe your fears or worries and then let them go, it helps to identify where your thinking is causing serious problems and where it is interfering with your emotions. We tend to take things related to emotions very serious even when it is not that significant. Mindfulness practice breaks this habit and removes the obstacles in our way.

Faith/Spirituality

Not every one of us is religious or spiritual, but humans generally feel the need to be connected to something bigger, something beyond us, and this is usually achieved in religion, meditation, fraternization or intimate relationships. Faith provides a way of coping with these obstacles, the belief that tomorrow is going to be better than today, and that the situation you find yourself is not permanent. Going to church, mosque or temples can connect you with a valuable support network, other faith groups can be useful, prayer can help, but the ultimate goal is to let go of the negativity around you.

Chapter 11: The Power Of Habits

If we want to embody what we learn about the brain, we must introduce new habits to make the new information we've discovered become part of who we are. Habits are what create us as we repeatedly do them over long periods of time. Habits can be very hard to break and most of the time they can only be altered instead of being extinguished completely. This chapter will look at what habits are and how they develop. We will show you how to construct new habits and alter old ones. We will guide you towards a life that is carefree and successful because your habits are pushing you in the right direction.

How Bad Habits Develop

Habits develop due a repeating a behavior over and over, usually for a period of at least 21 days. Many of us have unconsciously collected bad habits over our lifetimes. When we are growing up, we look to members of our family and our friends in order to determine how to live. The problem with this is that sometimes we replicate the bad habits that are family and friends are engaged in without realizing they are actually bad. Examples of this include talking about other friends behind their backs. Of course, when you reach adulthood, you know that talking about people behind their backs is wrong. But as a child, you do not possess the same awareness and you will most likely engage in the activity if all your friends are doing it. As humans we are very easily influenced by the actions of others and we often look to imitate.

Habits are a necessary part of human evolution. They allow us to learn things which we can begin to do unconsciously while our brain focuses on other important things. Without learning the habit of walking, we would be unable to walk and talk as we would have to have our complete focus on the muscles, we use to move our legs. Some say that 90 percent of our thoughts and actions are subconscious which means they were built out of habit. This is a startling statistic and it shows how important it is to really look closely at what habits we do have and make sure they are serving us well.

The Habit Loop

All habits work in a three-step loop. The steps are cue, routine, reward.

Cue: The cue is the trigger that sets the habit in motion. For example, making a cup of tea for yourself may trigger your urge to get a biscuit.

Routine: The routine is the automatic behavior that follows the initial trigger. This may be you going over to the cupboard to find a packet of biscuits.

Reward: Finally, you will get some form of reward for completing the routine. This may be the taste of the biscuit as you dip it in the tea or the relaxing feeling you associated with having the two items together.

The brain is only active during two periods of the loop. When the loop starts, the trigger engages the brain to tell it what habit to use. When the loop ends, the brain is rewarded for the performance of the routine and this helps to solidify the connection between the cue and the routine.

Breaking bad habits

When habits are reinforced over long periods of time, they become very difficult to break. The best way to try and change a habit is by changing only the routine and keeping the cue and reward the same. For example, if you are trying to stop having biscuits with your tea, your best chance is to substitute something else for the biscuits. Preferably something healthy provided the reason you want to avoid biscuits is that they are unhealthy. So once your tea is made you go and grab some carrots and hummus instead. Then when you sit down with your tea and snack, you will still get that good feeling of relaxation you get from having tea and a snack.

Trying to completely eradicate a habit can be done but it is very difficult. The best way is to substitute out the routine. If you do wish to break it completely however you will need to do a lot of work to understand the root cause of the habit. You must be able to understand why you are doing it. Are you smoking because you like the taste of smoke or are you smoking because you feel stressed? If you are smoking when stress is triggered a great substitution would be to go outside and do one minute of deep breathing exercises. If you want to eradicate the habit however you will have to try and control your stress levels before they get too high. This may mean incorporating a regular meditation practice into your mornings or taking on less responsibility at work. You can see that when we look closely at our habits the root cause can often seem completely unrelated to the actual habit.

Bad habits you should change

Here we will talk about some of the common habits people have that limit their potential in life. If you wish to effectively rewire your brain and optimize your life it is important to get rid of these bad habits before you start trying to incorporate new ones. While the process of switching your habits may be difficult initially, once you get your good habits up and running for a month or so it becomes very easy. After all, habits become automatic so you don't even have to think about doing them!

Procrastinating

Many people spend hours each day procrastinating about all the work they have to do. Procrastination often happens as a result of having a huge mountain of work ahead of you. The trick to overcoming procrastination is to break down your work into manageable chunks. This allows you to attack it in small bites rather than trying to swallow it whole. We will use an example to illustrate how you could potentially change a habit of procrastination. Let's say you have a 10,000-word essay to complete by the end of the week. You still haven't started and there are only four days left to submit it. The problem is that every time you go to begin you aren't sure what to write (this is your trigger). So instead you click onto

Facebook and check if there are any updates (this is your routine). You see you've got a message from a friend about a party at the weekend (this is your reward). Now to change this habit, the next time you don't know what to write, jot down 200 words of whatever comes to your mind. Once you reach 200, then you can check your Facebook messages.

All we have done here is change the routine for when you feel stuck and we've kept the trigger and reward. By changing the routine, you are managing to get words on the page and the more you do this the more momentum you will gain. You may even push your routine out to 400 or 600 words before rewarding yourself next time.

Perfectionism

Perfectionism can turn into a limiting habit when it stops you from getting things done. It is almost always better to get something finished than it is to get it perfect. Most perfectionists start projects that never get completed as there is always more to be added or fixed. If this is a habit you have you may want to discover what the root cause of the habit is. Did you once complete something that wasn't perfect only to have it scrutinized by someone else? Did this cause you to fear to do things that aren't perfect? Whatever the root cause is, it is important that you no longer let this habit control your life or hold you back from doing great things in the realms or your work or career.

Lying

People tell lies for many reasons. Sometimes it is to protect themselves and other times it is to protect others. Inevitably though, getting into a habit of lying is detrimental to your relationships While it is debatable that certain white lies are ok now and again, habitual lying causes you to become untrustworthy. Trust is the most important factor in a relationship and without having a trusting personality most of your relationships will be false and unfulfilling.

Apart from lying to others we often lie to ourselves. This may be telling ourselves that we are happy in our current job when we really are not or that we don't see the need to change any aspects of our character when we know deep down that our confidence is not real.

Bad sleep

Most people do not get enough sleep for their mind and body's needs. Most of us need in the region of eight to nine hours of sleep to be functioning optimally, apart from a few outliers who can be effective with less. Try to break the habits that lead to you not getting enough good quality sleep. One such habit is looking at a screen before bedtime. The blue light from phones, TVs, and laptops blocks the release of melatonin which is a chemical that helps to indicate to our bodies when it is time to sleep. You should avoid the use of screens at least one hour prior to bedtime. If you can't manage this then try purchasing some blue light glasses that lessen the amount of blue light entering your eyes. Other things you can do to improve your quality of sleep include meditating, journaling, keeping the room at the right temperature and exercising early in the morning.

Phone addiction

Another bad habit many people have developed these days is an addiction to their smartphones. This can use up so much of your free time and attention which will ultimately stop you from focusing on the important things you should be doing to reach your goals. One tip to reduce your phone usage is to cancel your phone's internet plan. This will mean you can't use your internet unless in Wi-Fi zones. If you want to take it a step further you could even cancel your Wi-Fi subscription at home. This will make your home a sacred space to relax and get work done. If you need wifi you can always visit a local café. Another tip is to track your phone usage with an app called Moment. This way you can see how many hours of your day you are wasting on your phone.

Being impulsive

If you have a habit of making impulsive decisions that you later regret, you may want to focus on practicing mindfulness. Impulsive decisions based on emotions tend to not always get a desirable result. Emotionally-driven decisions can hurt other people and lead to poor relationships. Practicing mindfulness and deep-breathing exercises will allow you to become more present when you feel the urge to be impulsive. You will be able to acknowledge your emotional reaction and choose to delay making a decision or taking action. Giving yourself that extra few seconds before acting can make all the difference.

Chapter 12: Best Mindset To Permanent

Change Your Mind

5.1 Where to Start?

Willpower. Heard of it? Merriam Webster dictionary defines willpower as energetic determination. Willpower is what helps us get out of bed in the morning and go to work, even though that is not a place most of us want to be. Nobody wants to spend 8 hours of their day cooped up in a cubicle doing a job they're not passionate about, but they do it anyway because they know that they have to and they don't have a choice.

Will Power- A Closer Look

Scientifically, there is a specific part of our brain called the prefrontal cortex that controls our decision making, our ability to plan for the future and make choices that benefit us in the long run. This part of the brain is located in the front of the skull behind the eyes. Studies have mapped the brains of those with weak and strong will power and have seen actual differences inactivity of this area of the brain. This little section of the brain could be thought of as the 'willpower muscle.' And it operates in much the same way that your other muscles do: if you do not use it you lose it! The good news is that, like a muscle, it can be rebuilt, retrained and strengthened.

Training the Willpower Muscle –Start Small and Build

If willpower is essentially a muscle, the only way to get more of it is to train over time. As we take small steps to go against our natural inclinations, we can slowly build up our willpower. If you struggle with writing academic papers, you could start small. Practice writing a page at a time, despite your feelings. Then two pages, then three.

If you struggle with making healthy food choices you could, by sheer force of will, eat one healthy meal a day, and work your way up to two, then three. You get the idea. As you train your willpower on these smaller tasks, it will become strong enough to tackle bigger and more complex challenges. If you aren't sure where to be building up your willpower muscle, or if you realize that you have a naturally weak willpower, a good place to start is by taking up a sport or going to the gym. The mind/body connection is a powerful one and training them together can have a synergistic effect. If you begin at the gym by walking a half-mile, then a mile, then jogging a little while, then running a 5 k, you will see progress in your physical strength as well as the strength of your willpower.

Remember the adage, 'A journey of a thousand miles begins with a single step.' Think of tasks that you struggle with regularly and break them down into smaller chunks. Practice flexing your willpower muscles by achieving one small chunk of a task. As we discussed in previous chapters, motivation will often follow these small steps to action and help carry you along.

Willpower: A Limited Resource

Willpower is beginning to look like the ultimate solution to our procrastination problem. It is something you can train up, unlike your emotions you can control it, and so there is no downside, right? Think about this scenario:

In the morning, your alarm clock goes off. Your brain says "Just 5 more minutes of sleep." Exerting your willpower, you counter with, "I MUST get up and go to work. I WILL do it." You begrudgingly get out of bed and go to eat breakfast, where you are faced with a choice. Pastry or oatmeal? Again, you will yourself to make a healthy choice. "I NEED to eat better. I promised myself I would. Don't even think about it that chocolate donut!" You eat the oatmeal, resenting each bite. In the first ten minutes of your day, you have already engaged in two battles of the will. It's going to be a long day.

Just imagining this scenario is enough to make one wary. There is a reason why. It takes a great deal of energy to go against our natural inclinations and exercise the power of our will. In the last decade or so, scientists started studying willpower and the idea that willpower is a limited resource. Scientist exploring this idea refers to it as willpower depletion.

One such study conducted by psychologist Roy Baumeister in 1996 tested the concept of willpower through what was called the Chocolate-and-Radish Experience. In this experiment, Baumeister enticed a group of test subjects with the scent of freshly baked cookies. They were then led into a room with a plate of cookies and a bowl of radishes. Some test subjects were asked to eat the radishes while others were allowed to eat cookies. Afterward, both groups were then given a complex geometry problem to solve.

The group that ate radishes gave up on the math problem twice as fast as the group that ate cookies. The scientists behind this experiment concluded that the subjects who ate radishes depleted their reserves of willpower in resisting the cookie aroma. When they attempted the math problem, they simply had less willpower left that the group who got to eat cookies. The big problem with wanting to use willpower to win the procrastination battle is that if you're going to spend your life fighting against your procrastination tendencies, just like in a real battle, it is only a matter of time before you tire out and fatigue. Because of this, very few people manage to successfully overcome procrastination through sheer willpower alone.

5.2 Tips for Effective Goal Setting

Goal setting is really different for different people. But most goals fall into two major categories. The first are goals that we have a 95% chance of accomplishing, simply because we've done it before. The second category is the goals where there is a 95% chance of not knowing if we will accomplish them, simply because we've never done it before, but we would like to anyway.

There is numerous advice on how to do goal-setting right. So in this chapter, we will explore not so much about how to set goals, but more on how to accomplish these goals. Our minds and our subconscious are set up to help us achieve goals that we sincerely believe are achievable. Here are some tricks that can help you in goal setting and goal getting:

Be A Dreamer, but Stay Motivated

Goals are materialized because each and every one of us is a dreamer. But in order to accomplish your goals, you need to do something about them and that takes self-discipline and motivation.

Your first trick is really a mind trick. Have a burning desire and a reason to achieve it. The path to achieving goals is filled with boredom, procrastination, anxiety, excuses, and difficulty. There will be so many times that you will try to talk yourself out of this goal. But to keep going, always remember the reason and the desire of why you wanted to attain this goal because this helps you stay on track.

Break it down

Break down your goals into mini-goals. Your brain probably knows you can't achieve enormous goals in an unrealistic timeline. So when you create your goals, give it a 24-hour cycle. Essentially, create mini-goals. For example, if your goal is to eat healthily- don't tell yourself 'Ok! I'm going on a 30-day gluten-free diet today!' No, it doesn't work that way. Instead of saying 30 days, tell yourself you will go for a 3-day gluten-free diet and move up from there. Your mini goals must be reasonable, sustainable and attainable within your 24 hour time period.

Do Something Every day

The more you work on your habits and create a routine, the closer you are to achieving your goals. You would naturally take some time off but if you do not take the first 7 days or first 30 days of your working on your goal, you will never create the momentum you need to drive you till you reach your desired target. The first 30 days of a goal is crucial- it not only shows people you are serious, but it also boosts your morale and drives to keep you going and sustain your goals well beyond your target.

Learn to adapt and adjust

As you go on daily achieving your mini goals and working towards your bigger goals, be flexible. Be willing to adapt to changes along the way. Make your mini-goals slightly difficult if you deem them easy. Or if they become too taxing, then make them easier. The main thing is to remember that if it is too difficult, you might end up quitting. If it's' too easy, then you are pushing yourself. Find a middle ground that is decent for advancement each day. For example, if you have set your mini-goals to do 30 pushups daily, by the time you are 2 weeks in your training, you might feel that you can do more. So challenge yourself and bring up the daily goal of doing 40 pushups daily.

Looking back for feedback, looking forward to rewarding

Feedback and reward are essential parts of goal-setting and goal-getting. On your journey to goal-getting, be bold to request feedback from the people around, especially from the ones you look up to. Give yourself a little reward once a week or daily for accomplishing your goals. Rewarding yourself can be as simple as putting a gold star on your calendar on the days you accomplished your goals, so something more elaborate like dinner on Saturday night. This reward giving is positive reinforcement. These little things are good enough to tell your brain that you are doing something right.

Schedule Slop Time

Slop time is when you do not need to focus on our goal. It is the time that you can allow yourself to cheat on it or not do it at all. We are humans and we are bound to do it anyway, so you might as well allow yourself that space to be normal humans. Allowing slop time is crucial because it prevents us from feeling dejected or get bored. Temporarily ignoring a goal for a short period of time (like during the weekend) is great to refocus your energy and do things better when you start the next week fresh. Just remember not to over-do it and don't make this a habit. Slop times are good if it is done once or twice a month.

Sticking to the small, boring stuff

Doing things on a routine can get you bored. That is an undeniable fact. Achieving goals isn't about celebrating each time you complete a milestone. It's about sticking to the daily, small stuff no matter how boring it gets. Get the fundamentals right then make it slightly difficult the next day so you are constantly challenging yourself. Keep doing it again and again till it becomes a habit. When it becomes a habit, you'll realize that you look forward to doing it and it doesn't take that much effort as it used to.

5.3 Rewiring Your Brain to Overcome Addiction

You can only know when to say no when you know when to say yes. In other words, you need to know what you want in order to know what you don't want to do. For this, you must be self-aware. There is a great strategy to achieve this self-awareness: the happiness formula.

When you bear the burden of your duties, it can be very difficult to act, because nobody likes feeling obliged to do something that he has not chosen to do. The Formula of Happiness was created to remove this weight: when the duties become not only choices but the best choices that can be made in that situation and at that time, to taking becomes the best solution.

Mind Over Matter – Is It Possible to Change Our Mindset?

Not only is it entirely possible, but more importantly, it is very doable. How many times in your life have you found yourself face to face with a challenge, only to feel like you want to give up so badly because it just felt too difficult to overcome at that time? Admittedly, giving up can often appear like the most tempting choice – sometimes the only choice –when you're faced with obstacles where you feel like you simply do not have the strength within you to overcome it.

There are two types of mindsets in this one – the growth and the fixed. If you're someone who has a growth mindset, you will find that personal development is at the core of your focus. If you have a fixed mindset, on the other hand, you'll find yourself seeking validation instead. This very simple distinction between the two mindsets is what separates successful individuals from the ones who constantly find life a struggle to accomplish even the simplest of tasks.

Individuals with a growth mindset are the ones who have achieved monumental success in their lives. The ones that we look up to and aspire to be, the ones who are successes in the industries that they command. More importantly, they are the ones who did not let procrastination stand in their way and hold them back. This is the one thing that sets them apart, and it was having the right mindset. That's all it took for them set themselves apart.

Individuals who have a fixed mindset will find themselves very often not excelling at much because they constantly find themselves either procrastinating or making excuses not to do something. They are subconsciously afraid of failure, and thus, they avoid challenges because they don't want to risk being disappointed. Although they want to achieve goals and ambitions, they lack the desire, the drive to do so, and find it much easier to procrastinate instead.

Cultivating the Right Mindset Starts Now

Mindsets are essentially the beliefs that you have about yourself and what qualities you possess. Some examples of this could be your intelligence, your personality, your strengths, and your talents. The difference in backgrounds, life experiences, beliefs and situations all contribute to the kind of mindset that you have right now. Think about your own mindset for a minute, what does yours say about you right now? What do you want your mindset to be moving forward?

The reason why some people appear to have the mindset that propels them towards success is that they have cultivated it. If you want to overcome procrastination, this is where you begin, right here. Your perception will ultimately become your reality, and if you believe it is possible to make a change for the better, your life will eventually be better. The battle to win over the mind begins at this moment, are you ready to take on the challenge?

The Happiness Formula

The happiness formula is a simple but very effective tool to always make informed choices.

It is a sequence of questions to ask yourself before taking action:

Write down a task you must do. For example, I MUST write this 20-page report for my boss.

Turn the "I MUST" statement into a question that starts with "I WANT." For example: "Do I want to write this 20-page report for my boss?"

If the answer is YES, DO IT!

If the answer is NO to ask yourself: "Am I willing to pay the consequences of leaving this task undone?" (For example, you could be scolded by the boss, or could be fired)

If the answer is "YES, I'm not willing to pay the consequences," then DON'T DO IT. You have decided that the consequences are less serious than the action.

If the answer is "NO", then DO IT, you have decided that the consequences of not acting are worse than the action.

You may ask yourself. How is this different than willing myself to complete a task? The answer is self-awareness. You became aware of your own procrastinating thought patterns and you confronted them. Instead of going into an energy-consuming battle were you forced yourself to do something despite not wanting to do it, you changed your emotions and therefore changed your will. You took control not only of the situation but of your own mind. This is a powerful accomplishment.

The Fence

To strengthen the ability to say NO, people need to be aware of their own thoughts and the mechanisms that lead them to procrastinate. To make everything easier, it is useful to recognize the typical words we use when we are procrastinating: "not yet...", "I don't feel like it...", "wait...", "you can do it later...", with the emotions that accompany them.

The first thing to do is to activate an internal "radar" to recognize when you start having thoughts of procrastination. Just focus the radar on the words we have already seen: "still 5 minutes", "I do it another time" etc. Observing your thoughts, you will learn to recognize the words you use to procrastinate.

The second is to learn to observe one's thoughts in a calm and neutral way, without judging them or reacting emotionally. Many thoughts are automatic, therefore out of our control. No need to fight them or oppose them. It is enough to let them pass without saying anything. You can start with lower mail situations and become familiar with your thought patterns and learn how to deal with them when they are not useful to you.

When you have learned to choose your thoughts, you will be able to build your mental enclosure. Within the enclosure, there are the conscious choices you've decided to follow. Outside there are temptations, thoughts of procrastination, friends who tell us what we want to hear, etc. And the fence is formed by the word NO, which defends like a wall, against misleading temptations and thoughts. You decide what thoughts you are going to let go through the fence.

How to Build Stronger Self-Discipline

How is it that those incredible individuals we often hear about (or sometimes know personally) manage to achieve so much in their life? How do they have the discipline to wake up earlier than everyone else each morning, stick to a strict, nutritious health and fitness regimen and even have time to read several chapters of an inspirational book or listen to a podcast? All before someone else on the opposite end of the spectrum, has even mustered the energy to get out of bed this morning?

How do you start building this kind of self-discipline too? The discipline that is going to take your life to the next phase of success, the way you should have done so long ago if not for procrastination? By following these techniques below:

What Do You Want to Change?

Procrastinators often have several habits in their life that they want (and need) to change. Otherwise, they wouldn't be struggling with procrastination, to begin with. This is what you need to do right now. Make a list of all the habits that you think are causing you to feel lazy, unmotivated, uninspired and procrastinate, and then next to those qualities, make a list of suggestions on how you would go about changing them. Focus on one habit at a time and start working on changing that. Once you're done, move onto the next habit and slowly work your way through the list. Look to other self-disciplined individuals as an example and see which habits you could start to emulate.

See Your Failures as Lessons Instead

Failures along the way are an inevitable part of success. Like a rite of passage. It is something that you must go through to make success and victory that much sweeter and more meaningful. Think of the failures you encounter along the way as lessons that are going to make you stronger, build your resolve and make you a more determined person. What doesn't bring you down, only makes you stronger at the end, and with each triumph, your self-discipline strengthens and grows.

Saying No to Temptation

This is probably going to be the most challenging phase for a lot of people. If temptations were so easy to resist, self-discipline wouldn't be such a struggle to accomplish. Here's where the power of no comes in again. Each time you say no to something that is going to tempt you to procrastinate, your self-discipline grows stronger. Each time you don't give in to your desire, you walk away a little bit stronger and a little more disciplined. So keep at it and keep the momentum going, this is how you're going to build your resolve over time.

Avoid Last-Minute Decisions

Leaving decisions to the very last second can often result in you making the wrong choices. Which is why you need to now start making it a point to decide on things the moment you know that there is a decision to be made. Putting off and procrastination the decision isn't going to make it go away, it is just going to delay the inevitable. Learning to make decisions as you go trains you to have better self-discipline along the way too. Like deciding not to be distracted by your phone for the next hour until you get a task done.

Or deciding ahead of time you are going to finish this assignment today no matter what and commit to doing it. Deciding on how many emails you're going to respond to today. Deciding on how many tasks on your to-do list you're going to complete today. All these little decisions along the way help make you a more efficient, productive person down the road with better control and self-discipline in your life. It minimizes the chaos and hectic-ness that comes with last-minute decisions too.

Self-Discipline is Part of Being an Adult

Nobody said being an adult was easy. We have to do things we don't always necessarily like, but you know what? We survive. Adults don't wait around for people to tell them what to do and what not to do. The beauty of being an adult is that we have a mind of our own, we take our lives into our own hands and we make choices and decisions for ourselves. As adults, self-discipline is the driving force that keeps us going, pushing us through those uncomfortable moments in life.

Remember waking up each morning and going to work scenario? That's part of being an adult. To train your self-discipline and build its strength, you need to push yourself to do the uncomfortable things you would rather not do instead of waiting for someone else to force you to do it. Taking that proactive step, that initiative to do it on your own is how you build your self-discipline over time.

Setting Smaller Goals

This is the key to start building a better mindset for yourself. Not only is this a great way to start cultivating a positive mindset, but it is also great for helping you overcome procrastination. When we set big goals and we fail to accomplish them, they can be a big emotional hit for many. Feeling discouraged, we lose the drive to keep on fighting and moving forward. Eventually, it becomes easier to procrastinate because we simply don't feel like facing another possible failure yet again.

You need to set small goals with smaller, more doable steps to accomplish these goals. This is a much better strategy because each time a goal gets smashed, seeing your goal materialize before you will fuel your belief that you can do this. It will make you want to do more, and eventually, your mind starts to believe you are capable of anything. When that happens, procrastination fades away and becomes a problem of the past.

Chapter 13: What Are The Benefits Of A

Positive Lifestyle?

Having a positive attitude is an attribute that enhances your daily life but how does it impact your overall health? Does it improve any other areas of your life and if so which areas? Here are some interesting facts about how positive thinking can change certain areas of your life:

Health and wellbeing

We know that having a positive mental attitude makes life more enjoyable, but have you considered the fact that it can actually add years to your lifespan? There are great benefits to cutting out negativity and overthinking but what are the physical health benefits you can expect to feel?

1) Boost your immunity: Studies have shown that your mental thinking can affect your immune system. Participants who display positivity and optimistic thinking had a strengthened immune

system. Participants who displayed pessimistic tendencies had a less responsive immune system and were more prone to illness.

2) Increased resilience: If you believe you can cope with whatever life throws at you then you will be better equipped to recover from actual traumas and crises. If you can remain positive when faced with tough times you will be able to recover from the ordeal quicker. Negativity will lead to longer recovery and greater stress.

3) Reduce stress: Positive thinking is the perfect way to manage stress levels and reduce the impact they have on health. The way you think impacts directly on stress levels and help our bodies avoid stress-induced conditions.

4) Reduce blood pressure: One of the greatest problems faced by people is high blood pressure that accompanies increased levels of stress. Removing anxiety and negativity will help you lower

your blood pressure and lessen the chance of heart disease.

So, what does changing your mindset achieve for your health? Basically, optimists live longer! Positive thinking can add years to your life!

Success in the workplace

If you can change the way you think you can also achieve success in your career. Imagine if all your perceived problems became opportunities and enabled you to progress. When you realize that all problems are solvable to some degree you completely change how you perceive obstacles. You will soon become a "go-to" person and will rise through the ranks of your chosen career.

Motivation boost

Positive thinking can give you wings! You will begin to realize that your personal goals are achievable and rather than wondering if you can achieve goals you will wonder when you will achieve them. You will also become appreciative of your surroundings and the company you keep. This realization will motivate you to block any negativity entering your personal space and interfering with your mindset.

Harmonious relationships

How many people remain stuck in toxic relationships just because the alternative seems much worse. Once you realize that being alone or single is not a punishment or unpleasant you will be able to let go of relationships that cause you pain and sadness. Your improved mindset will attract a new type of person. This is known as the law of attraction when "like attracts like" and can bring joy and happiness to your personal relationships. Your close friends and even your partner will benefit from a positive mental connection and your relationships will thrive. Knowing that you can share your dreams and innermost thoughts with those that you love, no matter what their reaction, is priceless. Losing the fear, we have of other people's opinions will free your mind to explore new options.

Create a better first impression

How do you think people perceive you when meeting for the first time? Do they see someone who is interesting and fun to know? Although you are not affected by negative thoughts your new positive attitude will give you the confidence to make a great first impression. People, in general, are drawn to friendly, kind and non-aggressive personalities and feel at ease from the first contact.

First impressions can help you develop in many ways. Expand your social circle, meet new dating options or simply get on better with your co-workers. Your family life should also benefit from your new attitude and any past disagreements can be cast aside and forgiven.

Improves focus and concentration

When you think positively you free up the part of your mind that would be held back by pessimism. When doubt creeps in and tells you that what you are trying to do is impossible then part of your mind is occupied with these thoughts. Dispelling the negativity means you focus all your energy on getting the job done.

Negative thoughts are energy thieves and steal away your peace of mind. Making the choice to think valid, positive ways to benefit yourself will concentrate your focus on achieving your goals. Your mind will clearly show you how to go forward and refuse to be hampered by indecision or doubt.

Happiness

The feeling of better health improved personal relationships and success in both personal and work-related goals can only lead to one thing. A happier you. The more value you place on your life then the happier you become and the more you enjoy life to the full.

Inner beauty

Who do you admire for their beauty and attraction? Ok, mean and moody film stars aside, the most attractive people in life are smiley happy people who seem to have an inner light that makes them glow. You will benefit from this inner glow once you rid yourself of negative influences. Your eyes will shine with hope for the future, your skin will glow from your healthier life and your smile will light up the room. Your posture will improve as your self-confidence grows and you will carry yourself with the bearing of a winner.

These benefits are only a drop in the ocean of the possibilities available to you. You have just dipped a toe, get ready to dive right in and bathe in the benefits that a positive mental attitude will give you. Optimism and positivity are the two most important skills you can possess and the only person holding you back is yourself!

Chapter 14: Overcoming Fear And Anxiety

Fear is one of our strongest emotions. It has an astoundingly strong effect on your mind and body.

Fear and anxiety can pop up for a brief period and pass only a moment later, but they can last much longer. From time to time, they can take over your life, affecting your ability to eat, rest, concentrate, travel, enjoy your day, leave the house, or excel at work or school. This can prevent you from achieving the things that you need to do or acquire the things that you need, and may, furthermore, impact your health.

Some people become overwhelmed by fear and the need to maintain a positive outlook about things that may make them startled or nervous. It will, in general, be hard to break this cycle. Be that as it may, there are multiple ways to do so. You will feel better if you learn healthy ways to deal with your fear; that way, you will not feel so overwhelmed by it that it doesn't keep you from living.

What makes you anxious or restless? Since anxiety is similar to fear, the strategies mentioned above also work well for anxiety. Anxiety occurs when fear is debilitating and endures over a prolonged period of time. It is connected to something that might or will happen in the future, rather than what's happening right now.

What do fear and anxiety feel like? When you feel frightened or nervous, your mind and body react quickly. Your heart may beat more quickly. You may breathe in extraordinarily fast, shallow breaths. Your muscles may feel weak. You may sweat a lot. Your stomach may feel queasy. You may find it difficult to concentrate on anything. You may feel frozen, cemented to the spot. You may not be able to eat. You may have hot and cold sweats. You may get dry mouth. You may get astoundingly tense muscles.

Over time, you may become depressed, experience trouble sleeping, develop headaches, have difficulty working and preparing for the future, have issues having sexual intercourse, and lose self-confidence.

These things happen because your body, detecting fear, is setting you up for an emergency, so it makes the blood in your body flow to your muscles and gives you the mental ability to focus on what your body sees as a threat. Furthermore, it may your elevate blood sugar.

Why do I feel like this when I'm in no real danger? Early humans required the fast, mind-blowing responses that fear causes because they were routinely exposed to physically dangerous conditions; regardless, we do not normally face comparable perils in modern-day living.

Regardless of this, our mind's bodies still work quite similarly to those of our early ancestors, and we have comparable reactions to our modern worries over bills, travel and social conditions. Nevertheless, we can't escape from or physically attack these issues!

The physical assessments of fear can be alarming in and of themselves – especially if you are experiencing them, and you don't have the foggiest idea why, or in case they seem, by all accounts, to be disproportionate to the situation. Instead of warning you about impending danger and setting you up to respond to it, your fear or anxiety can kick in when it perceives very dangerous or slightly dangerous. These situations could be imaginary or minor.

Why won't my fear go away? When will I feel normal again? A small amount of fear is normal when you are faced with something new. Or it could be a faint, slightly intuitive fear about someone or something, even though you can't put your finger on why. Some individuals feel constant fear and anxiety, with no particular trigger.

Understanding Panic Attacks

An anxiety or panic attack can be referred to as a time when you feel overwhelmed by feelings of fear and exhibit the signs mentioned earlier in this chapter. People who have attacks of nervousness often complain that they have difficulty breathing, and they worry that they're having a heart attack or will lose control of their bodies.

What is a Phobia/Fear?

A phobia is an over-the-top fear of a particular animal, thing, place or situation. People with fears have an amazing need to avoid any contact with a specific explanation behind the cause or fear. Coming into contact with the explanation behind the fear makes such a person with phobia fretful or panicky.

HOW CAN YOU HELP YOURSELF?

Face your fear if you can.

If you, by and large, avoid conditions that you are afraid of, you may stop achieving the things that you need or want to do.

You won't have the chance to determine whether your fears regarding the situation are valid, so you may miss the opportunity to learn how to manage your fears and lessen your anxiety. As a result of being overly cautious, your anxiety may increase, Facing your fearful emotions and attacking the underlying causes can be a suitable technique for beating your anxiety.

Know Yourself

Get acquainted with your fear or anxiety. Keep an anxiety diary by jotting down your fearful and anxious thoughts when they occur. You can try setting yourself small, reachable goals for standing up to your fears. You can write down a list of things that you can look at now and again when you are most likely to become frightened or anxious. This can be a feasible technique for observing the beliefs that are behind your anxiety. Keep a record of when it happens and describe what happens.

Exercise

Exercise requires some concentration, and this can take your mind off your fear and anxiety.

Relaxation

Mastering relaxation techniques can help you to deal with the mental and physical feelings of fear. These techniques can help you to relax your shoulders and help you to improve your breathing. You may imagine yourself in a relaxing spot. You can also try alternative methods for relaxation, such as yoga, meditation, and back rubs.

Avoid Excessive Food Intake

Eat lots of fruit and vegetables, and avoid consuming too much sugar or sugary foods. Too much sugar consumption increases blood sugar; this can lead to feelings of tension. Try to go without drinking an excessive amount of tea and coffee, as caffeine can increase anxiety levels.

Avoid or Limit Your Consumption of Alcohol

It's normal for some people to drink when they feel fearful. Some individuals call alcohol 'Dutch guts', yet alcohol can make you feel progressively anxious or tense.

Complementary Medications or Alternate Strategies

Some individuals find that complementary medications or exercises, for example, relaxation strategies, meditation, yoga, or tai chi, help them to deal with their anxiety. You can select whichever of these strategies that you prefer to win over your anxiety.

Chapter 15: How To Break The Rerun Habit.

Interrupt the rerun. Not just once but often! You are trying to develop an new way of thinking or a habit. Try a simple one word trigger- "stop!" whatever you choose to do to interrupt the rerun, keep in mind it takes time to develop a habit... once will not be enough!

Focus on your body. If you pay attention to your thoughts when you're rehashing an old argument, you'll likely notice that you are breathing shallow and your muscles may be tense. By focusing your attention on how your body feels and taking an few deep breaths, you'll be able to draw your attention away from the old conversation and into the present.

Take time to figure out why you're hooked on over-thinking. Over-thinking isn't something you're born doing. It's a habit you formed over time, probably as a defense mechanism to the possibility of failure. Look at your thoughts critically and ask yourself if there are certain situations that trigger mental reruns and if, in the grand scheme of things, is this really so important? Will you still care a year from now?

Put pen to paper. Next time you find yourself beginning a mental rerun of a conversation or event, try instead writing it down in a journal. In doing so, you may find it much easier to identify underlying issues, or to simply let go of the experience, and become aware of how unhelpful such thinking is.

If you find yourself hooked on over-thinking old conversations and dwelling on the injustice of it all, thinking about what you should have said or done, without taking any corresponding action, you risk increased feelings of stress and unhappiness. Life is simply too short to waste reliving yesterdays…. Remember that no matter what happened in the incident you keep recalling, you're a human being worthy of love and respect.

OVERCOME OVERTHINKING AND STEP TOWARDS AN IMPROVED LIFE

So let's say you are hanging about at a gathering, surrounded by colleagues and clients, and you happen to have spotted someone you really want to talk to. Maybe its business related or you just want to build up personal ties. Whatever way it is, you prepare an mental draft of what to say, as one does and intend to go meet them but a tingling fear in the back of your head stops you in your tracks. What if they do not want to converse with you? What if the particular line of conversation does not work out? Or even goes horribly wrong? Your fear creates a sort of domino effect, and you begin to think of the worst that could happen as the inevitable. With each thought you are pulled deeper into the tangled mess of confusion inside your mind, and this ultimately, renders you unable to even talk anymore. You then watch as another person engages in a conversation with the subject: an opportunity lost.

Overthinking and the consequent restlessness and anxiety, while proves to be a huge deterrent in one's social and personal life, is also surprisingly common and for every person who is a victim to it, becomes the cause for opportunities lost and moments that one would later regret. But with an few daily practices and a determined attitude, it can be overcome easily.

Acceptance

The first step towards dealing with excessive over thinking and anxiety are accepting the problem in the first place. Only after this would, you be able to go ahead and solve it. But while knowing that you a remunerator is important, it is also vital that you realize that you are not alone in the situation and that there is no reason to panic. Over thinking is a normal thing among a lot of people today and you would be able to overcome it with a positive attitude.

The Best Moment Is The Present Moment

The best thing you can do about over thinking is obviously to stay with the present. Your brain can't think of faraway matters if it's busy where is should be with the flow. You also learn to appreciate your surroundings, and being in the present completely improves your performance on any kind of task significantly. And although it is much easier said than done, there is an few methods which you can exercise daily to minimize the cycle of negative thoughts to a great extent.

One good example is breathing. You will be surprised at how much this helps. Just close your eyes and take deep beaths for a couple of minutes. Closely watched, and taking deep breathes help to pull you in the current moment and aids in clearing your head.

Another good example is meditating to practice mind fullness. The basic idea is to remain silent and simply focus on all that is around you closely, and this has worked wonders for am lot of people. Just once a day, just close your eyes and try to take in all your surroundings. Listen to your thoughts but do not 'interact' with them, and eventually you can try to turn down their 'volume'.

In addition to that, slow down. Do everything you do with full awareness of you doing it. Try and narrate to yourself every step that you make, and force yourself to notice your surroundings. This will also help you to stay in the present moment.

Be Confident

When full to the brim with self esteem and feeling good about yourself, you build up a positive mind-set. You would find yourself to be less prone to overthinking, and so everything that you do or say turns out to be done better. One of the first things you can do is get busy. Form a plan of what to do for the day, and keep being productive.

Doing things keep your mind from wandering off, and in addition to that, getting stuff done results in a great boost in confidence through a sense of accomplishment. You should also try and do something you're really good at least once a day. Whether you're an expert at playing an instrument or you possess extraordinarily talent for a video game, take some time off from your schedule and do it. It'll be a great help.

Another life altering change you can make is to fake it. This might sound hard but this actually works great. Pretend that you're a character you know, who is witty, smart and sure of themselves. Perhaps you know one from a television show, an movie or a book. Go ahead and deliver everything you say with confidence, even if you are not sure of it, or you are terrified. You is will find that as you fake it more and more, eventually, you inherit that confidence in real life.

Let go

Trying to control all the outcomes of your life is undoubtedly the main cause for remuneration. Because when you do, you are also doomed to feverishly think of what to do in every moment of your life in fear of what could consequently happen next. The best thing you can do is to convince yourself not to. Realize that you have no say in what happens in your life, and this there is no reason to worry about it. The universe has your fate decided, so you should just make the most out of every moment. Try and realize this before anything you might be hesitating to do and it'll help you to stop overthinking and just do it.

Another thing you can do make specific time frames to make any decision. Whether it is to go and talk to someone or bigger life choices which might be forcing you to overthinking. Take a minute for the little ones and an few days for the larger ones in life at the most. This would push you to assess a decision rationally and research to make the best choice possible. Once you do make a decision, steel yourself and just do it. It might be frightening but you'll find it rewarding at the end.

At the end of the day, the most important bit to realize is that we all hold the potential to achieve everything we have dreamed of, and the only thing we have to do is to steel ourselves and remove our deterrents. And that makes all the difference

Conclusion

In this book, overthinking and its underlying related mental conditions, including anxiety, worry, depression, and fear, are explored with focus placed its beneficial role in our lives. Armed with an understanding of the root components of overthinking, the reader is made aware of when overthinking becomes a problem. The serious consequences of overthinking are specially made clear to the reader, so they can identify it when it shows up, especially its paralyzing and delayed effect on decision making. Next, the causes and solutions to overthinking and its underlying mental conditions are covered, which include changing one's perspective, socializing with loved ones, engaging in relaxation techniques, therapy, self-love, and acceptance.

Psychology concepts such as the law of attraction and self are also explored in this section of the book. After that, there is an emphasizes on the importance of positivity and positive thinking to shift one's mindset away from a negative and self-destructive one. The book ends with an encouraging message that urges the viewer to be themselves and go with their heart in life.

Overall, this book is an exploration of human psychology, especially our insecurities, anxieties, and stresses, as well as a guide to solving it. It hits close to home because it tackles mental health conditions that many of us struggle with and attempts to make some sense of it in the modern world. Ultimately, in order to overcome overthinking and its underlying mental conditions, one must be willing to change themselves and reach out to others, most importantly. Self-improvement is something that requires mentors and support in order to accomplish; else, a person feels isolated, giving them no reasons to leave their minds and become a part of society.